PROSPERITY, PEACE, RESPECT

How Presidents Have Managed The People's Agenda

Elizabeth Warren, Ph.D.

authorHOUSE®

AuthorHouse™
1663 Liberty Drive, Suite 200
Bloomington, IN 47403
www.authorhouse.com
Phone: 1-800-839-8640

© *2009 Elizabeth Warren, Ph.D.. All rights reserved.*

No part of this book may be reproduced, stored in a retrieval system, or transmitted by any means without the written permission of the author.

First published by AuthorHouse 4/10/2009

ISBN: 978-1-4389-6220-7 (sc)

Library of Congress Control Number: 2009902240

Printed in the United States of America
Bloomington, Indiana

This book is printed on acid-free paper.

To Kathryn

Contents

PREFACE

The Twentieth Century saw some of the most dramatic events in American history: wars, depression, great political movements, and powerful social change. Many Americans remember important parts of that history and see that the election of 2008 was a turning point in many ways. Americans are looking very seriously at their country, wondering what they and their new government can do to deal with a damaged economy, the requirements of a realistic foreign policy in a world plagued with hostilities and terrorism, and the need to make right the wrongs of poverty and racial hostilities still present among our own people. This book seeks to understand the background of these three issues to discover what changes one hundred years' development of the country has produced in them and what our Presidents have contributed to that development.

Societies do not progress in a straight line or even in a predictable pattern, but there are lessons we can learn from economic stresses, threats from other nations or peoples, and social hostilities among our own people. There have been panics before, and recessions that go with them. Unemployment of large numbers of people has been endured before, although no one thinks it is a tolerable condition for any length of time. There certainly have been wars that posed severe threats to the United States; the Second World War began with devastating attacks on our shipping in both the Pacific and the Atlantic. For an example of poverty and unemployment we need only look at the Great Depression of the 1930s with its 25% jobless rate. As for hostility between racial groups we despair at the degraded legal and social status of black people in our country for several centuries before a measure of justice was enacted. It is reasonable to ask the question, is our system adequate for the problems we must solve?

We have come through a time of serious trial in the 21st Century. After an attack on our people by an international outlaw group, we have seen seven years of a Presidency that, out of fear for the nation's safety, has bypassed some fundamental human rights, rules of law, and the need to keep good faith with the people. All of our professions of justice and democracy state that we are governed by the rule of law, that we respect the rights of all, that no one charged with a crime can be convicted and punished without due process of law. While it is true that we as a nation have not always practiced that which we profess, we have believed in it. We believe in individual rights and freedom. We thought our structure of government the most likely to secure to our citizens the blessings of liberty. As a people we have thought that we always have tried to improve our system and ourselves.

All of this sounds so idealistic as to be unreal in today's world. We are beset by terrorists who act at will against any nation or people. We are reminded regularly by them that they think the American lamp of freedom is a sham, that we will attack another nation at will, pre-emptively, in order to get what we want in the way of resources like oil. We have incarcerated some 300 prisoners at Guantanamo Bay, Cuba, and continue to hold them as "enemy combatants" without charge of any crime. We have engaged in torture of some prisoners, contrary to respected international law. We continue in a war although probably a majority of our people want us out of it. It's not just that we want our men and women in the military to come home; we feel stuck in the wrong kind of war and have a great sense of shame and guilt because of our continuing presence in Iraq. Then there is Afghanistan where we did identify the enemy and attacked it. Then we left the job unfinished. We want a leadership that tells the world we have come to our senses, we are a people that believes in justice and human rights. At the same time, we have to deal realistically with terrorists around the world. It helps to realize that Presidents in the past have dealt with similar serious crises, and this was especially true during the World Wars and the Cold War. How did they deal with their crises?

We seek perspective on our troubles, looking to the recent past in order to gain a clearer understanding of where we should go. What has happened to our better nature? Have Presidents often sought means, legal or otherwise, to strengthen their positions as they confront a crisis? Whatever will we do about the interest groups, the lobbies?

Because I think you may be as interested as I am in political leaders and how they have dealt with the nation's stresses, I have devoted this book to 20th Century Presidents and their challenges. We will review their perceptions of their political environment and their policy choices based on that understanding. We'll see some of the people they have worked with and depended on.

With this perspective we can talk about Presidential leadership, seeing it through the eyes of leaders who reacted to stresses on the nation and sought means to control them, all within a democratic context. Not an easy task.

AGENDAS AND POWER

The American political system rests in an environment full of agendas brought by important people. It consists of agendas from the past as well as the present. It consists of the President's agenda and includes the agendas of Congressional leaders, bureaucratic agencies, court judges and justices, and interest groups. Not to mention State and local governments and foreign governments. It's all about power and how leaders use it in dealing with the agendas.

The Framers of our Constitution intentionally set up an arrangement wherein power would be divided. Moreover, the entities they created -- the President, the Congress and the Supreme Court --were enmeshed in checks and balances, so that each one could exert limits on each of the others. Thus, the President can check the Congress by proposing laws. He can use the "bully-pulpit," his State of the Union message and other addresses to persuade Congress and the public to support his proposals. Members of the House of Representatives, with two-year terms, are always running for election. If they are members of his party, they watch to see if their local publics support the President or not, and they have to decide whether they agree with him on controversial issues. The President also has the power to call them into special session in a national emergency. He is responsible for seeing that the laws are faithfully executed. The Supreme Court can declare the acts and decisions of either of the other Branches unconstitutional.

The Congress was dealt with in Article One of the Constitution because the Framers intended that the peoples' representatives should be the primary decision-makers in the United States. Congress has the power to legislate for the nation, and if the President vetoes a bill, Congress can over-ride it. The legislative body also can investigate the actions of the Executive Branch, perhaps its strongest power because it publicizes the results of its investigations, and this can have positive or negative implications for the President and his appointees. Enter the Bureaucracy, people appointed to a wide array of government offices beginning with the Cabinet officers and going through independent executive agencies and the independent regulatory agencies. These agencies have numerous subordinates and the Bureaucracy has significant influence on the decisions of government.

In spite of its specifically enumerated powers, Congress over the years gradually lost pre-eminence to the President and the Supreme Court. The Framers intended that the co-equal branches of the national government should cooperate with each other or else would be set against each other so that each could check some important actions of the other two. The President has the power to appoint justices to the Court and all federal courts, but the Senate can refuse to approve an appointee. The President can make treaties but the Senate has the power to either ratify or reject them. The Congress has the power to declare war, but the President has the power to deploy the military forces of the nation, and Presidents have done so without a specific declaration of war by Congress.

The separation of powers and the checks and balances system set up by the Framers was intended to create countervailing forces in order to prevent an accumulation of power in any one person or branch. But the system does not quite work as the Framers intended. Instead, the presidency developed over time through the interpretation of the powers delegated to the President, and because of the requirements of wars in the Twentieth Century, the office has become more powerful than the Framers intended. Arthur Schlesinger, Jr's book *The Imperial Presidency* explains in detail how this happened.

If all it takes to set up a government is an arrangement of powers and checks and balances, the United States would be a different kind of country. Following the prescribed organization, the government the Framers created would have caused frustration at every turn and the leaders could not have acted together in the public interest. Instead, the leaders of the young republic found that they had to organize supporters to advance their various proposals. Thus political parties developed out of a need to grease the wheels of the branches of government. Another thing that helped, of course, was money. In addition to the state banks, a bank of the United States provided a means for people to invest in the future of their country and the national government could assist in the travel westward of pioneers who wanted to carve out a home and a new way of life in the wilderness.

Today, the Executive Branch of the American government is a sprawling group of departments, agencies and commissions charged with administering the vast reach of a congeries of public policies. Most of these agencies are scattered throughout the United States. The policies of the government at any given time are the accumulated laws adopted by Congress, the directives issued by the Executive Branch, and especially by the President, and the decisions of the federal courts including the Supreme Court. These policies were made by the wisdom of leaders past and present. Their tendency is to maintain stasis, that is, the status quo. Most Presidents reach the highest political office in the land by promising the electorate that they will bring some change to the vast governmental apparatus, and many people vote to advance the changes they want. Typically, however, governmental policy changes only slowly and incrementally over the years. Government policies change significantly only when society itself changes; sometimes that occurs with a great upheaval like the Civil War in the 1860s or the economic dislocations of the Great Depression of the 1930s, or the Civil Rights movement of the 1960s. At other times, the pace of change is likely to be glacial.

It is in this context that Presidents and Congresses must use the instruments of government to sustain a satisfactory living environment for its people. There are many issues our Presidents must address; this book discusses three of them: the economy, foreign policy, and social stresses. In the Twentieth Century Presidents and Congresses have dealt with the disruptions of an industrializing society, including two world wars, economic busts after boom times, the social impact of racial inequalities, and the expectations of changing population cohorts. They have had to manage a revolution in communication, and radical changes in weaponry after the development of atomic power. Not only have we been adapting to these remarkable inventions, but our scientists have developed drugs that perform wonders to treat diseases. Such benefits are eclipsed, unfortunately, by the advent of viruses or bacteria that survive and overcome the effects of some drugs, leaving their victims no better off than they were before they were when the illness attacked.

Humans strive for perfection both spiritual and material, and it is always heartening the degree to which human intelligence can improve the condition of mankind. Government in the United States is expected to support progress, restrain or regulate those who take advantage of others who cannot compete, and punish those who violate the law. Society is always imperfect, however, and if we take into account the acquisitive nature of Americans and their love of freedom, we can appreciate how our government must struggle to keep control of our domestic condition while continually striving to protect us in an unruly world.

It is in this context that we ask the question how have recent Presidents dealt with economic recessions, depressions, or runaway booms. Each of the Presidents in the Twentieth Century has had to deal with the variable economy of the country or decide to do nothing about it. Going to other issues, how have Presidents reached the decision to use military forces to cope with attacks on the United States or threats to the nation's interests around the world? Were there decisions to not act? What did Presidents decide to do about social upheavals of one kind or another in the Twentieth Century?

As part of our picture, we must take into account what kinds of people we have elected to the highest office in the land. Each president is temperamentally different from others. Each has a background that forms his personality, his reason for seeking the office, his skills and weaknesses, and his ability to relate to people. His responses to problems may differ from those of his predecessors although past decisions can give guidance to those in the future. However, scholars have observed certain characteristics of leadership that may give a President success in his efforts. He (or she at some time in the future) has a grasp of the economic and social conditions in his country and he fashions programs to enhance strengths and ameliorate problems. He is able to communicate what needs to be done so that people will follow his lead. He is able to organize a party of followers from a variety of economic and social groupings in the country. He intuits what measures will be acceptable to the public and what will not. His proposals will be those that the public believes in or at least will tolerate. He understands the philosophical ground of the society, what it believes, to what degree it will unify under his leadership. He must have courage and good judgment.

Questions about the economy, foreign policy including war, and social stresses help us focus our inquiry on each of our Presidents in the Twentieth Century as we assess how they have responded to crises and issues that have shaped this part of the history of the United States. Thus we can gain some perspective on the future management of our country in the Twenty-first Century.

THE ECONOMY IN 1900

The economy of this country has been a preoccupation of leaders in government since colonial times. How have the people earned their living and how have they organized their society? Early in our history, people earned their living by farming or crafts in wood and metalworking for all kinds of needs, and mining for materials to make implements to support this kind of work. Ship-building in the northeastern colonies created the essentials for trade up and down the Atlantic coast and in the Caribbean. Planting and harvesting cotton and later tobacco with slave labor was the economy of the South. Trade with England and European countries was a subject of hot dispute between the mother country and the colonies and helped precipitate the revolt by the American colonists. By the time the Constitution was approved, the States had adopted currencies, banking, trade and State and national laws to regulate these relationships.

What kind of philosophy should govern a relatively simple agricultural economy like this? America looked to its forebears in England and Europe for some kind of governing philosophy. Adam Smith, a Scot, inquired into the nature and causes of the wealth of nations and wrote his book.[1] His key ideas: self-interest and competition drive men. Smith had studied the political economies of several European countries seeking to understand what caused wealth and what caused poverty. Free trade, competition and choice, he discovered, would encourage economic development and reduce poverty. Therefore, an economy based on those principles would improve the moral and social condition of mankind. This economic philosophy suited American buying and selling and early manufacturing to a T.

We remember the development of an industrial society from our history books; we had pictures of the final spike being driven to connect the cross-continental railroad tracks. We learned of new ways to produce faster the goods that people wanted. The first Sears Roebuck catalogue books provided an easy way to buy clothes and household items like furniture using the mails. We learned of the first telephones becoming available, and we heard about the excitement of the Columbian Exposition in Chicago in 1893 demonstrating the electric light, and showing how electricity could drive other household appliances too. The telegraph, the automobile and other wonders, were transforming the United States at the beginning of the Twentieth Century.

The westward movement of Americans in the 19th Century and the settlement of that vast expanse of land, much of it arable, fostered a state of mind that was independent, self-reliant. People felt that if they could move freely, then settle and build a cabin or house and farm the land, they could provide a living for themselves and their families. From this attitude of self-sufficiency, people could build communities and new social networks that would enhance the self-help. Life was very difficult at first, of course, and many pioneering families did not survive the brutal winters in the northern territories or the severe drought that might occur unexpectedly almost anywhere. An assured source of water had to be available in the new towns as well as the means to get it to farmland and household. Sketchy local governments had to be created to protect settlers against marauders, Indians and wild animals. The federal government provided the protection of the U.S. Army to help protect the settlers and other means to enable people to expand the nation. After the Civil War it promoted agriculture through land grant colleges in what were then the Western territories.

By the end of the 19ᵗʰ Century, the population of the country had grown exponentially as immigrants from European countries and the Far East who wanted to start afresh traveled to the United States. A Civil War had been fought and won over slavery not only on the question of emancipation but also because the South's economy had been based on slavery, a situation that became increasingly incompatible with the economy of Northern States. Once that changed, there were changes in the nation's economy. By 1890, the American economy had absorbed the beginnings of industrialization, and new sets of relationships were emerging. Manufacturing plants employed increasing numbers of workers, often at low wages, with long hours of work, and dangerous working conditions. By the 1890s, workers were protesting that government should step in to provide them assurances of a minimum living income and tolerable working conditions. They demanded that government provide security for workers to organize for the purpose of bargaining with industry owners or managers.

The public philosophy of these years was laissez-faire in the economic sphere. The key ideas were belief in the free enterprise system and competition, and these were backed by generations of independent-minded Americans. The ideas found strength in Adam Smith and his economic philosophy. In the face of these beliefs were serious struggles between labor and the captains of the industries where the working people made their living. People were expected to take care of their own, their families and themselves. The fact that conditions in an industrializing country generally did not favor such a positive attitude toward work in industry was of less importance. So workers found ways to express their outrage at the unfairness of the economic system. They organized strikes in the face of the law that wouldn't allow strikes and would only bring on the police.

In 1860, the Englishman Charles Darwin published his *Origin of Species.* His book and theory upset many established beliefs about the natural world. That human beings could have evolved from apes was a frightening idea for many people. While Darwin never intended that his findings and his theory of evolution, which included his idea of the "survival of the fittest," should apply to a person's ability to support himself in society, that idea crept into the thinking of some American theorists who were devoted to the notion of individualism and a laissez-faire economy. William Graham Sumner,[2] a Yale professor of social and political theory, was one such observer of British scientific thinking, and Andrew Carnegie, the American owner of a steel industry, was another. The American view stressed the importance of the individual's responsibility to support himself; government should have no role in the relationships between industry and the laboring man. The fit will survive and prosper and the human race will be the stronger and better for it. Thus Darwin's idea about evolution in nature was picked up and used to explain the economic survival of people. The theory is referred to by historians as "Social Darwinism." It is an idea that Charles Darwin had nothing to do with.

The "Social Darwinism" idea was pernicious. As America industrialized, there were always people at the bottom of the economic ladder whom employers could use at will to advance their private incomes and those of their industries. There were no protections for industrial workers in matters of working hours required, wages paid, or child labor used unless an owner wanted to attract workers by providing such benefits. Moreover, industries competed with each other on a cut-throat basis, or were absorbed by another to dominate a market. The laborer was usually outside the scope of business relationships.

Socialism and Communism

In this context, more Americans became aware of European socialist and communist ideas about the condition of the laborer in an industrializing society. Socialism, the idea that government should acquire and operate the means of production, namely the major manufacturing industries and perhaps others, all for the benefit of the people was advocated by socialists in Britain, like the Fabian Society. But the Fabians also thought that the changes in capitalism should happen gradually, and they did not advocate revolution. George Bernard Shaw and Sidney and Beatrice Webb, leading Fabians, discussed and wrote about their views around the turn of the century.

Karl Marx in his *Communist Manifesto* (1848) and in *Das Kapital*, (1867) with Friedrich Engels, stressed their belief that the capitalist classes of the industrial countries were exploiting their workers and that governments would always support the capitalists. Thus there would be no justice for workers; the only thing they could do to help themselves was to stage a revolution against capitalists and overthrow the government that supported them. Then they should create a government of the proletariat.

Marx saw capital accumulation as destructive of the working class where Adam Smith had seen it as the engine of economic growth. Marx, like Adam Smith, was concerned with the value of labor and how that could be measured so that a working man could be paid fairly for his work. Both Smith and Marx would agree that people pursue their self-interest, but for Marx this was grossly unfair for the working man. Wealthy men could accumulate more and more wealth, in terms of money and land, and what others owed them. There was only so much money to go around. The thought that the use of capital could generate new growth was not in Marx's calculations. Where Smith saw the wealth-creating possibilities of free trade and competition, Marx could only see the degradation of the working man. Thus, while Smith thought capitalists should be encouraged, Marx called for revolution. The working classes, the proletariat, should revolt against their masters, the capitalists, overthrow the government that supported them, and install a dictatorship of the proletariat.

Marx said that capitalism creates a proletariat and believed that there was an automatic process in history called the dialectic: thesis, antithesis, synthesis. The thesis was capital, the antithesis was labor, and the two were engaged in a mighty class warfare. With the proper leadership, a revolution would occur and the proletariat would win, overthrowing capital and creating the synthesis, a classless society. To deal with the huge changes in the society, you had to have a government structured as a "dictatorship of the proletariat" for a time. Then, as a natural course of events, the state would "wither away" and a classless society would emerge. There would be no government, just the "administration of things."

Government Regulation

Regulation of some aspects of the American economy was not new by the latter half of the 19th Century. There had been regulation by the States and by the Federal government earlier in the Century in matters concerning commerce. The Constitution provides that Congress may regulate commerce "among the States" and use of the waterways was one form of commerce. There were objections to the regulations, of course, but they were not about whether regulation was proper under the Constitution, but rather which jurisdiction, State or federal, should be controlling, and whether the regulations were fair to those concerned. In 1887, the Interstate Commerce Commission was created to regulate the railroads. As the nation grew and industrialized, the Congress and the I.C.C. established regulations for all kinds of transportation in the United States for more than one hundred years. The I.C.C. was abolished in 1995 in a wave of deregulation.

Economists identify two forms of regulation in this country: economic regulation and social regulation. Some instances of regulation, however, involve both. For example, wherever fairness is involved, both economic and social issues are important. Regulating the rates that farmers had to pay to ship their goods for sale to various parts of the country was economic regulation in the 1890s, but it also involved the issue of fairness to an important segment of the national economy, agriculture. Without regulation, the railroad industry could exploit the farmer. Similarly, when the government finally acted with force to regulate industries in their relationships with labor, such as pay, hours worked and safety conditions for workers, this concerned both the economy and the social benefits that would accrue to workers. The right of workers to bargain collectively with management for the terms of their contracts was another form of both economic and social regulation. An example of what economists call social regulation would be the civil rights legislation of the 1960s when a number of laws were passed to stop racial discrimination in schools, voting, public accommodations, and housing. Every one of these had economic effects and again both forms of regulation were intended. The Civil Rights Act of 1964 was based on the commerce clause of the Constitution: many places that accommodated the public were in interstate commerce – hotels, restaurants, all manner of facilities.

Another form of regulation entirely was anti-trust, the purpose being to prevent monopolies which were believed to obstruct competition. This was economic regulation and it had the effect of keeping the market open for anybody "who could build a better mousetrap." In 1890, Congress passed the first of several anti-trust acts, the Sherman Anti-Trust Act. In 1914, the Clayton Anti-Trust Act succeeded the Sherman Act and was adopted during the Wilson Administration.

Adam Smith's theory was that free competition among the small businesses that existed in the late 18th Century promoted wealth in the countries he studied, while if government regulated trade, a country would not prosper but be poor. The assumption of anti-trust legislation was that if companies were forced to compete with each other, they would perform better in all ways, in their product and in their treatment of workers, who could work somewhere else if they were unhappy. And if a company did not perform well, the "survival of the fittest" rule would apply.

There were no rules, however, that could prevent gigantism in an industry. Even when large industries like the railroads, the oil companies, the steel companies and others at the turn of the Century could not form monopolies, they could and did grow and at that point the question of monopoly came to be based on size alone. In a 1920 decision dealing with the U.S. Steel Corporation, the Supreme Court decided that that company was not a monopoly even though it controlled more than half of all steel production in the country. It did not engage in "unreasonable" restraint of trade, said the Court.[3] This raised the question of market share, a question which the Court decided twenty-five years later, in 1945: ninety percent of market share would be monopolistic.[4]

These examples illustrate the difficulty of defining terms and making judgments about the fairness of the market for large companies and small. The Twentieth Century experience with large companies posed new questions about doing business in the United States. By the end of this Century, a revolution in regulation had occurred in a wave of "deregulation." But that is ahead of our story.

THEODORE ROOSEVELT
1901-1909

If ever an American President personified the mood of the nation, Theodore Roosevelt was he. At the beginning of the 20th Century, the energetic T.R. came into office after the nation had recovered from the devastating Civil War, and had endured the economic boom and bust cycle in the '80s and '90s. By 1900 most of the Territories on the continent had become States. The Union which Abraham Lincoln had struggled to preserve was a reality even though first class citizenship for blacks was not realized for another seventy years with the Civil Rights Acts. The nation was full of optimism and expectation. How could it be otherwise with the advent of electricity for one's home, the automobile, telephones, the telegraph and even the airplane? The belief in progress, which had fed the westward expansion, found its strength again with all of the new inventions.

As a child, young Theodore Roosevelt was sickly, suffering from asthma. His wheezing struggle to get his breath kept him and his parents awake many nights until he reached his teens. Change of climate did not help. Eventually, around the age of twelve, his father told him that he would have to build himself up physically. Teddy determined to do just that, and began a vigorous program of exercises at the gym and on an apparatus on his own back porch. After the year of physical exertion, the asthma was much improved, attacks came less often, and he was not seriously threatened by that illness for the rest of his life.[1]

Theodore also loved to read books; in many respects he was self-taught, particularly about the natural world. He built a collection of bird skins that interested naturalists in later years. He also had an excellent formal education. Theodore's love for his family expressed itself in superlatives: "My own darling little Motherling" and "My dear Papa." Brother Elliott "is a noble fellow, wonderfully grown up in every way" and "I wonder if ever a man had two better sisters than I have!"[2]

Thus, the young T.R. grew up to be the antithesis of the sick child. His victory over asthma led him to believe that a vigorous life with disciplined exercise would resolve any physical weakness. Moreover, this was accompanied by an exuberant love of life. His interests encompassed nature, history, and politics. The powers of the presidency were both an intellectual challenge to him and an emotional magnet. In many ways, he was among the happiest Presidents ever to serve the United States.

For a man whose love of his family was so real and his enthusiasm for life so full, the death on the same day of his wife, Alice Lee, and his mother were staggering blows. Scarcely recovered from this tragedy, he decided to wind up his business in the New York Senate and go West. He had gone into the cattle business in the Dakota Territory in 1883, and now went back to the Bad Lands to pursue his interests as a rancher and hunter. It was a rugged way of life where a man of his background received no respect but rather was thought of as having a weak moral character because he wore glasses. Roosevelt overcame this stereotyping with a fist fight and a few well-chosen words.[3] His energetic response to frailty or sorrow stayed with him throughout his life.

Roosevelt had developed a professional career after Harvard and law school. He had been elected to the New York Senate in the early 1880s, so when he returned from the West, he wasted no time resuming his political career. He served as the Police Commissioner of New York where he was known to walk the streets at night to watch for criminals.[4] He was appointed to the first U.S. Civil Service Commission in the '90s, a job that he loved because of its dedication to finding qualified people to serve government outside of politics. He was elected Governor of New York in 1898 and two years later was elected to the office of Vice President of the United States on a ticket with William McKinley for President. He waged his own campaign as the nominee of the Republican Party while McKinley stayed quietly in his Ohio home town. T.R. became President when President McKinley was assassinated in 1901. He was re-elected to that office in 1904 running for his own term.

In these years at the turn of the Century, there were serious struggles between labor and the industries where the working men made their living. A poor living it was, with low wages, very long working hours and in some cases dangerous working conditions. People were expected to take care of their own, their families and themselves. The fact that conditions in an industrializing country generally did not favor such a positive attitude toward work was of less importance. So the working men found ways to express their outrage at the unfairness in the economic system. They organized for strikes in the face of the law that wouldn't allow that, and would only bring on the police.

Roosevelt was still in the Dakota Territory in 1886 when a peaceful strike in Chicago became particularly violent. On a cold day in May, strikers from the McCormick manufacturing company held a rally in Chicago to bring attention to their urging for an 8-hour workday. Police were sent in to protect strikebreakers, and this aroused anger among the strikers. They called for a rally the next day, and a large number of workers came to demonstrate in favor of the 8-hour day. This rally became violent when someone threw a pipe bomb into the ranks of the police who had been summoned again to keep the disturbance down. Several policemen were killed or injured and in the melee, several workers were also killed. The police arrested eight of the workers in the belief that there were anarchists among them. These people were tried, convicted, and 7 of them were executed for their presumed crime, the eighth was imprisoned for life. Legal reviews of the court's decision subsequently concluded that the trial was unjust.[5] No one knew who threw the bomb. The court's handling of the cases reflected the panic that had spread throughout the city. T.R. was horrified by news of the Haymarket Riot. It offended his sense of order, and he could get just as angry at workers as he could at the captains of industry for allowing such disorder as a strike turned violent.

The Economy

The vigor with which the President approached all issues emerged in his dealing with the economy. His philosophy was based on his belief that there needed to be a balance between the forces at work in the economy. Some of his friends were industrialists but he could countenance no favoritism if friends were involved in economic disputes. Roosevelt believed that personal morality was required of everyone, and he considered that he should manage those elements in the economy that needed correction.

Roosevelt himself was convinced of the salutary nature of personal struggle and he also embraced laissez-faire as the backbone of the American economy. He focused much of his economic policy on promoting a balance between business and industry on the one hand and labor on the other. For example, he thought the economy was threatened by the railroad industry which charged high rates to ship agricultural products and other merchandise around the country. Roosevelt called for railroad rate regulation to be administered by the Interstate Commerce Commission to regulate the maximum rates. He struggled with leaders of his party in Congress in the crafting and the passage of the Hepburn Act in 1906. The Speaker of the

House, a rock-ribbed Republican from Indiana named Joe Cannon, thought that Republican T.R. was some kind of maverick, and used his position to slow the President's initiatives about rate regulation of the railroads. In this frustrating fight, the President showed his ability as a political leader. The legislative package he proposed to Congress had included tariff reform intended to improve trade relations with the Philippines, but that, together with his push for rate regulation was more than Speaker Cannon and the Republican leadership in the Senate could stomach. The President would back and fill to get movement on his proposals, knowing when to give in to the opposition and when to insist on his own position. Roosevelt saw that he would have to give up the tariff reform effort if he was to get the rate regulation through Congress. So that's what he did.[6]

T.R. was a very popular President but while the Republican leaders in Congress welcomed the popular support he had all over the country, they were prepared to resist him on matters of concern to the old guard. In a case similar to the railroad rate issue, the President became outraged that the Standard Oil Company, with a near monopoly of the nation's oil pipelines, was overcharging customers in New England hundreds of thousands of dollars a year and did this "by unfair or unlawful methods."[7] The pipelines were in interstate commerce, and should have been subject to regulation by the Interstate Commerce Commission, he thought, and this was overcharging. Senator Lodge, from Massachusetts, secured the issue for the President, and for his own constituents, by drafting an amendment to the Hepburn bill classifying all pipelines as common carriers, hence subject to I.C.C. regulation.

Roosevelt's view of his own role as President stemmed from his patrician background and his conviction that the nation needed help. There was an element of noblesse oblige in it but it was more than that. He saw it as a function of dispassionate leadership to secure justice where there would be no favors for either industry or labor.

21

"President Theodore Roosevelt and Family"
1903 Library of Congress digital ID cph.3c13665

If his peers who were captains of industry did not act in keeping with proper morality, he must step in. He thought the nation's economy was threatened by the excesses of big business on the one hand and the insistence of working men that they were being treated unfairly on the other. To add insult to injury, they thought government was helping business in that treatment. TR earnestly sought a balance between the dominance of industry and the growing protests of laboring men. The means he sought was regulation of industry. An important part of his thinking about government was that it should favor no class, that it should in fact be classless, with honest, dispassionate political leadership and with objective civil service administration of the regulations necessary to secure justice for all.

There were other important economic issues that the President decided had to be dealt with. As the press and the public became increasingly aware of the abuses by all kinds of industries, Roosevelt acted to resolve them. In *The Jungle,* Upton Sinclair described dramatically the practices of the meat-packing industry, artistically conveying the smell of spoiled meat which was, nevertheless, packed and sold to markets where people bought their food. Around the same time, the President read articles by Lincoln Steffens about the conditions of slaughterhouses and meat-packing plants. Moreover, the proliferation of patent medicine being sold around the country was also in need of regulation. The Pure Food and Drug Act was the outcome of public exposure in books and magazines of practices like these and the President's pressure on Congress to act.

As he sought to bring balance to the economic forces in the United States, T.R. exhibited his personal distaste for disorder. He thought the nation was threatened by a lack of order and discipline. Thus, while the "muckrakers" like Sinclair and Steffens published books and articles supportive of Roosevelt's goals, he deplored muckraking quite publicly.[8] He feared that the nation's industries could lead it into chaos, an eventuality ripe for extremists on both right and left. Had not McKinley been assassinated by an anarchist? Were not radicals in Europe publishing ideas about a proletarian revolution and the destructive character of capitalism? There were socialists also in this country, like Eugene Debs, who had gained attention from reformers. The idea of reform itself became an issue for the President. His programs for regulation of industry were adopted by a Congress that was often resistant, but well aware of the tenor of public discourse about abuses of the laissez faire system.

The President thought the Supreme Court was in the pocket of the industrialists but there was little he could do to affect their decisions unless a vacancy occurred. However, very gradually, in the early years of the 20th Century, the Supreme Court came to modify its view of the relationships between industry and labor. In Lochner v New York (1905)[9] appellants brought a case that argued for the 8-hour day in certain industries. The Court turned them down stating that the contract clause of the Constitution was controlling. The subject industries could determine the hours that employees should work. But three years later, in Muller v Oregon, a judgment about a ten-hour work day for women in laundries reflected a change in the mind of the Court.[10] This and later cases were brought by lawyers who explained the effects on people of certain practices by industry. What happened to women who worked long hours in a laundry? Stress, fatigue, illness, and these conditions should not be tolerated for women who were the child-bearing part of the population. Louis Brandeis argued the case for Oregon, and this was an early example of "sociological jurisprudence," a basis for deciding cases that includes examination of the effects of a law or decision on people's health, safety and welfare. Brandeis' argument won the case for Oregon; the State could regulate the hours women could work in laundries.

Theodore Roosevelt's work to balance the forces in the economy that appeared threatening to the public peace as well as the health and safety of the people were probably his greatest accomplishments as President. He was challenged by some members of Congress who favored the status quo, by the Supreme Court and the current understanding of the law, and on the other hand by appeals of those who could not defend themselves against the powers that ran the economy. He worked his way through the problems by compromise when necessary, but also by vigorous use of the bully pulpit when he thought it necessary.

Foreign Policy

Roosevelt's foreign policy developed in the debates about the building of a canal through Panama to connect the Atlantic and the

Pacific Oceans. He wanted to strengthen his country economically and maintain its dominance of the Caribbean. To this end he entered a discussion about such an isthmus that had been going on for many years in Washington. The engineering plan had been prepared by Ferdinand de Lesseps and the original agreement, the Clayton-Bulwer Treaty of 1850 signed by the United States and Great Britain, to build an isthmus to connect the Atlantic to the Pacific Oceans through a Central American state, had been opposed by American nationalists. A new treaty was signed, the First Hay-Pauncefote Treaty in 1900, whereby the United States would build and administer the canal but it would not be fortified and would not be closed in time of war.[11] At that time, T.R. was Governor of New York, and, like many of his countrymen, he opposed the treaty too unless the United States controlled it in both peace and war. He thought this was necessary in view of the importance of American sea power and a proper observance of the Monroe Doctrine. This was the President who said, "walk softly but carry a big stick."

Soon after he came into office in 1901, Roosevelt urged the Senate to ratify a Second Hay-Pauncefote Treaty. It did so, but Britain refused, then later relented and approved a second draft of the Second Hay-Pauncefote Treaty which incorporated provisions sought by the U.S. Senate. Thus the way was cleared for the construction of the Canal, though it took years and many worker deaths in the doing. It finally opened in 1914.

While T.R. achieved admirable success in mediating between Russia and Japan in 1905 to end their war and bring a stable peace, and mediated among European powers to resolve a dispute concerning French Morocco, these were signal victories from events that were not threatening to the United States. In both cases he was asked to step in, and for his efforts he was awarded the Nobel Peace Prize in 1906. The public generally was pleased that he had been thus recognized.

The social stresses evident in the first decade of the Twentieth Century were those between labor and industry. The strikes and the increasingly intense demands by laboring men were part of the economic picture that Roosevelt tried to correct. But certainly, race issues were important. Roosevelt invited Booker T. Washington to a social event at the White House and in other ways tried to show respect to Negroes who were organizing to give themselves a place in American society.[12] The National Association for Colored People was founded formally in 1909.

Roosevelt wrote in his Autobiography "When I left the presidency, I finished seven and a half years of administration, during which not one shot had been fired against a foreign foe. We were at absolute peace, and there was no nation in the world. . . whom we had wronged, or from whom we had anything to fear." [13]

WILLIAM HOWARD TAFT
1909-1913

Seldom have we had a President who did not want the office. Taft did not want it. An experienced lawyer, he wanted to be appointed to the Supreme Court. He had been serving as a Federal Circuit Judge in Cincinnati. Then later he was appointed by President McKinley to serve as Governor, the chief civil administrator, for the Philippines. T.R. appointed him to be Secretary of War during his second term, and urged Taft to run for President in 1908. Nellie Taft, his ambitious wife, drove him to it. Taft liked Roosevelt, considered him a good friend and was dedicated to accomplishing the important work begun by the Roosevelt Administration, but he did not function the way T.R. did. He was more an administrator than a political operative. At the urging of the President, Taft was duly nominated by the Republican Convention, but he did not like campaigning at all. His Democratic opponent was William Jennings Bryan, who had run for President twice already and campaigned vigorously. In spite of his lack of enthusiasm, Taft won handily because of the vigorous support by Roosevelt. [1]

William Taft had a serious physical problem: he was obese. The problem had been with him as a boy. One biographer explains his overeating as a psychological reaction deeply imbedded in his personality as compensation for a sense of inadequacy.[2] His parents, particularly his mother, expected much of her children and William was in many ways a model boy at school. While as President he did not perform as well as Roosevelt, Taft was a victim of his own exaggerated self-criticism. In time, he would retreat from his surroundings and sleep sitting up at meetings in the White House; a large lunch would contribute to his drowsiness. He would take long trips through the nation primarily to get away from the White House and the demands of his office. He was a warm and friendly person and perhaps too sensitive to tolerate the criticism a President endures. He would take long vacations.

President William Howard Taft
Oil on canvas, Anders Leonard Zorn, 1911,
courtesy White House Art Collection

Politically, Taft was a conservative and his appreciation of the law made him view the Presidency legalistically, not politically. He did not try to expand the powers of the Presidency as did Roosevelt, and unlike, T.R., he thought that much of the needed progress to stabilize the economy could be accomplished using the law and normal procedures. Taft's skills lay in administration, as his record in the Philippines showed. There, he helped the people build their economy, build roads and schools. He and his team prepared a Criminal Code of Procedure, a general incorporation act, an Internal Revenue Act, and regulations for the sale of land. He prepared a legislative districting act so that the country, then still a Territory, could elect a Legislative Assembly for its governance. Taft was especially appreciated by Filipinos because he replaced the military governorship of General Arthur MacArthur.

The Economy

Without fanfare, President Taft fulfilled a role usually attributed to T.R. as the nation's number one trust-buster. The Taft Administration brought 80 antitrust lawsuits during his four years in office. One of these was against the U.S. Steel Corporation. The Justice Department charged the Corporation with monopoly, a combination of smaller steel companies, and this action was in violation of the Sherman Anti-Trust Act. Ironically, when Roosevelt heard about the lawsuit he was angry because he had supported the joining of Tennessee Coal and Iron Company to U.S. Steel in 1907. The action by the Justice Department made T.R. look duplicitous, for he had a well-deserved reputation for opposing monopolies.

The Congress, meanwhile, had adopted the Payne-Aldrich tariff bill raising tariffs on imports. The President was convinced that the country should engage in foreign trade. But there was considerable disagreement in the country and in Congress as to whether tariffs should be lowered or raised. Protectionism was strong in Congress, as personified by "Uncle Joe" Cannon, Speaker of the House. Taft tried to talk the conservatives into choosing lower rates, but the conservatives were too strong. A compromise was finally achieved among the legislators so that tariff duties were reduced on a few items but were left high on many. Taft had threatened to veto a high tariff bill, but finally he could not do so. He did not want a fight.

Taft believed that there was a need for a Federal income tax, but he thought simple legislation would not do; a constitutional amendment was necessary. This issue had been discussed for many years, and the Supreme Court was brought into the act in 1895 when it decided that such a tax would violate the Constitution because it was a direct tax and would have to be apportioned according to the populations of the several States.[2] This case was argued on the laissez faire sophistry that had no basis in the existing conditions of the country in the 1890s. The nation needed substantial new money to carry out its programs, and legislators recalled that a temporary income tax had been levied during the Civil War. The proposed constitutional amendment, interpreted as an "indirect tax," was approved by Congress in 1909 and sent to the States for ratification. The Amendment was ratified in 1913.

Taft also supported the direct election of Senators, later approved by constitutional amendment. These issues were both part of the program that the Progressives wanted adopted. Another important accomplishment of the Taft Administration was that federal government employees were given the eight-hour work day.[3] While this was good for the employees, it was also a very good model for industry as a whole. Nevertheless, the eight-hour day was realized for industry only many years later.

A breach developed between Taft and Roosevelt as the result of T.R.'s displeasure with his successor. He may have believed the conventional criticism that Taft was asleep on the job. But actual differences in philosophy emerged: Taft's conservatism and Roosevelt's progressivism. Taft decided to run for a second term in 1912 because he thought he should do so and because he was feeling better about his own achievements in the office. The Republican Convention, controlled by the Old Guard Republicans, nominated him, but not until after the Convention had endured a tumultuous several days of charges and counter charges. Roosevelt, running against Taft for the Republican Party nomination, had won the California primary election, but the credentials committee gave the two seats which were contested to Taft.[4] Ultimately, it was clear that the Old Guard controlled the Convention and was choosing Taft. Roosevelt, who called himself a "bull moose," walked out of the Convention and staged his own Bull Moose Convention which launched him as the Progressives' candidate for President. Had it not been for the split in the Republican Party, Taft may have won re-election, but because Roosevelt drew many Republican votes, Woodrow Wilson won the election.

Taft was happy to return to the law in spite of his loss at the polls. He became a Professor of law at Yale University and it was from that post that he was appointed by President Warren Harding to be Chief Justice of the Supreme Court. He was thrilled by his appointment which had been truly his heart's desire all his life.

THOMAS WOODROW WILSON
1913-1921

Woodrow Wilson is revered as one of the great leaders of the Twentieth Century. He presided over some major changes in the economic role of government in American society, such as the income tax amendment and the legislation creating the Federal Reserve Act and the Federal Trade Commission. He continued the effort of his Republican predecessors to further control the trusts with the adoption of the Clayton Anti-Trust Act. Finally, his conviction that the nations engaged in a dreadful war in 1914 should ultimately frame a peace with collective security to prevent future wars, indeed did change the world. The Senate rejected it in 1919, but the concept was restored after the Second World War with the creation of the United Nations. Lesson learned: America could not isolate itself from Europe nor from other nations. The world had changed after another brutal war was brought on by a madman who persuaded the German people that the Treaty of Versailles was designed to punish Germany, and she would have to fight to restore her place in the world. She needed "lebensraum", space, and access to the sea.

Wilson's leadership urging a league of nations was appreciated by world leaders through the 20th Century. Far from being a lost cause, which it seemed to be in 1919, Wilson's struggle proved a benefit to Europe and increasingly to Third World countries. The Eastern and African nations have their own roles to play in the United Nations, and while that body's structure frustrates those who have to deal with the differences among nations, it is nevertheless working its way through difficulty to provide collective security where there was none before. Only a delicate balance of power among the great nations, which included empire-building, defined their relationships for centuries.

Wilson's father, a Presbyterian minister, taught Tommy a religion that was comprehensive, so that as he grew older he could grapple with the tumultuous period the country had recently gone through, the Civil War and the financial panic of the 1890s, and at the same time develop his own thinking about the future of the country. As the young man grew to maturity, he determined that he wanted to study politics, and somehow be a leader in government.

Wilson achieved many of his objectives in spite of the fact that he could not read until he was ten years old. As a child, he had what today is called dyslexia though his parents thought Tommy was just slow. Then, when he was able to put together the written word with the words his father spoke in preaching sermons,

> (He) perceived letters and words as possessing a mysterious power, a power not easily captured and the more potent for its elusiveness and mystery. When he finally did decode the alphabet and enter the priesthood of the literate, he felt an exhilaration that stayed with him his whole life.[1]

The biographer, H.W. Brands, said the boy when he could read found something almost akin to magic in words and sentences, and particularly the ideas they enabled. Wilson delighted not only in reading but in speaking. He would practice making speeches in his father's empty church, developing an imaginary audience that appreciated his wisdom, and this helped him when he studied humanities and writing.[2] At Davidson College, he came to realize that writing and oratory were his favorite interests and they were the skills that led him into politics. He entered the College of New

Jersey (Princeton), where his father had attended seminary, to finish his formal education.

He took courses in government and politics, gradually organizing his ideas about government and society. He saw the relationship between individual citizens and their government as a covenant, like the covenant honored by the Presbyterian Church. The American Constitution was a covenant with the people in his view. He also did not see individuals as a collectivity but as single individuals. His economic theory conceived of business enterprise as composed of individual entrepreneurs, but they had an obligation to act in behalf of the public interest. He had read his Adam Smith and believed in the laissez-faire view of government with regard to business. Competition should govern the marketplace. However, in his later years he came to see the importance of regulation by government in certain activities of commerce such as banking and the fair distribution of, for example, electricity as a public resource. Wilson conceived of society as being a holistic entity. Everyone should fulfill his responsibilities, including people who led large businesses, but if there were areas where competition became unruly and the benefits of the market were not fairly distributed, government should act.

After Princeton, Wilson entered law school at the University of Virginia but found the study of law boring. It was a two-year program; he stayed with it eighteen months, then left. His father urged him to continue with the law, but Woodrow escaped often to read history and politics. He entered the practice of law in Atlanta, but found it unrewarding, and he felt he was not suited to it.

He heard of a new university founded by Johns Hopkins in Baltimore, and he applied, was accepted, and from there was able to pursue his interest in government, particularly the American Congress. He wrote his dissertation, *Congressional Government* and from that point was launched on an academic career. He taught the theory of government at Bryn Mawr College and Wesleyan College in Connecticut, and finally went back to Princeton to teach. He continued to be engaged in writing books and articles and became a very popular teacher. His reputation by this time, 1902, was substantial and he was much in demand as a teacher and speaker.

The University was undergoing a change in leadership at this time and it sought out Wilson for the Presidency. He accepted, having been offered that post at several other universities as well. His years as President of the University gave him a national reputation not only as an academic but as a speaker about the things he considered important in American society and government. He was dedicated to both the arena of ideas and the arena of public service, and wanted students to serve their country. It was he who coined the phrase, "Princeton in the Nation's Service." From Princeton, he went on to become Governor of New Jersey and in due course, he ran for President.

Woodrow Wilson, Author: National Photo Company ca 1913-1920,

Wilson came to the Presidency with a well-developed concept of what a leader should be and how government should work. His sense of his covenant with God, his dedication to duty, wholeness, integrity, work, and justice served him well through all the stresses he sustained. He understood that serving as President involved the exercise of power, but he thought of this as the power not to coerce but to persuade.[3] On Inauguration Day in 1913, he commented to one of his aides that it would be ironic if he had to deal much with foreign policy, because he had no experience of such matters.

The Economy

As President, Wilson wanted to fulfill the role he thought a President should take with the respect to the legislative body. He had long considered the Congress as the primary branch of government, in keeping with the intention of Article I of the Constitution. His *Congressional Government* spelled out how he thought of that relationship. He wanted to work with Congress to enhance the activity of competition in the business of America. He made this clear in his first address to Congress:

> "We must abolish everything that bears even the semblance of privilege or of any kind of artificial advantage, and put our business men and producers under the stimulation of a constant necessity to be efficient, economical, and enterprising, masters of competitive supremacy, better workers and merchants than any in the world. . . The object of the tariff duties henceforth laid must be effective competition, the whetting of American wits by contest with the wits of the rest of the world."[4]

In his first two years in office, the President and the Congress produced the tariff reduction bill he sought, the passage of the Sixteenth Amendment which gave the government the power to levy an income tax, and the Federal Reserve Act which created a central banking system with private ownership under the supervision of the government. The Clayton Antitrust Act of 1914 was a successor to the Sherman Act of 1890 which was not strong enough to penalize some practices of monopolies. The purpose of the Federal Trade Commission Act, also passed in 1914, was to allow the Commission to specify what practices were to be considered unfair.

Wilson was a States' Rights Democrat. He did not see the States as disruptive of the body politic, even though the Civil War had shown the disastrous consequences of independent thinking among the States concerning economic matters. Lincoln had fought for the Union, and Wilson considered the Union as the embodiment of the covenant which was the Constitution. Later, in his adulthood, Wilson saw and used the values of leadership to bring about the desirable end through government. Certainly, as President, he exerted his skills to lead the Congress and the nation toward many of the goals of the Reform Movement, as it was called in the early 20th Century. Wilson thought of himself as a conservative. Scholars call him a Cleveland Democrat, but his later espousal of many goals of the Progressive Party, which had been formed in 1912 in preparation for the election campaign of Theodore Roosevelt, seemed to suggest that he was a reform-minded politician.

While Theodore Roosevelt visualized something like a New Nationalism for the United States; Wilson spoke of a New Freedom. During the period of stresses on the economy in the 1890s, new conceptions of the relationship of property to human welfare recognized that a concentration of industry was inevitable. Reformers saw a form of justice that conservatives did not see: a concept of social justice. They wanted the government to control big corporations and protect and encourage the worker. This is a dynamic democracy, they thought, and it had to be susceptible to change.

Wilson thought of social justice in terms of his idea of liberty, of freedom. He wrote,

Human freedom consists in perfect adjustments of human interests and human activities and human energies. . . Life has become complex ; there are many more elements, more parts, to it than ever before. . . the individual is caught in a great confused nexus of all sorts of complicated circumstances, and (that) to let him alone is to leave him helpless as against the obstacles with which he has to contend . . . without the watchful interference, the resolute interference, of the government, there can be no fair play between individuals and such powerful institutions as the trusts. Freedom today is something more than being let alone. The program of a government of freedom must in these days be positive, not negative merely.[5]

Wilson, true to his southern upbringing, saw freedom as political liberty available to all Americans, but he did not see Negroes as struggling for their position in society. If the "program of a government of freedom must in these days be positive," his concern for free people did not include blacks. He removed them from government jobs, a decision that kept them out of government jobs until Herbert Hoover made those jobs once again available to blacks. In this matter, Wilson differed from Theodore Roosevelt who understood the struggle of blacks and tried to encourage their leaders.

Although both Roosevelt and Wilson were committed reformers, seeing the same dangers for ordinary Americans, the same unfairness, they came to the problem with somewhat different solutions. Both believed in the value of competition among businesses. They did not have the same view about the States, however. Wilson believed in the proper governmental role of the States; T.R. saw them as often the vehicle the special interests used in appealing to the courts to protect themselves. Nevertheless, the thrust of the Progressive Movement expressed many points upon which both Wilson and T.R. could agree.

War and Foreign Policy

Wilson viewed with horror the war that had broken out in Europe in 1914, after the murder of an Austrian arch-duke. America had avoided any involvement in European affairs throughout the 19th Century, and Wilson was unprepared to engage the Europeans. He declared America's neutrality. While the war raged, he was concerned with his legislative program. When he campaigned for a second term in 1916, he stated his intention to keep the nation out of the war. This sufficed for a time, but soon the parties to the conflict began to look for resources to continue their battle, and they sought money from the United States to be obtained by the sale of French bonds. The Secretary of State, William Jennings Bryan, the dedicated populist, was not inclined to assist bankers in any event, and the President wanted there to be no question about the neutrality of this country. So at first, the French initiative was turned down. Before long, however, the President's position was undone by normal financial activities between the United States and the Europeans.

German submarines were prowling the waters near Britain; indeed one torpedoed and sank the British liner Lusitania in the Irish Sea in 1915. On board were some 128 Americans in a total of nearly 1200 deaths from that attack.[6] Germany had declared a war zone to exist around the British Isles, and warned that any shipping entering that zone could be attacked, even ships from neutral nations. This event and the threat put the United States on guard about Germany. In time, its submarines became a sufficient threat to this country that the President felt compelled to ask Congress for a declaration of war. The President called for a draft law to build an army, an unpopular move that was challenged in court. But the challenge was rejected and the President continued to mobilize the country for war. Wilson's Secretary of War was Newton Baker and his general for the expeditionary force in Europe was General John Pershing.

Wilson delivered a speech to Congress making fourteen points about the post-war world and how the issues of concern to the belligerents should be dealt with. These would include absolute freedom of the seas, open covenants openly arrived at, self-determination for colonial peoples, territorial settlements in Europe and the Ottoman Empire, and a "general association of nations" which would provide guarantees of territorial integrity for all nations.[7] The British and French leaders, notably Prime Minister David Lloyd George of Britain and Premier Georges Clemenceau of France, were quite cool to Wilson's idealism. The Germans, however, saw in Wilson's position a way to reach an armistice between belligerents without surrendering. By June, 1918, there were one million Americans in France, and they continued to flow in. The German army had staged a major offensive and lost to the British and French, so Germany was looking for a way out. Here, Wilson had an opportunity to broker an armistice and after several months, that is what was done.

The British and French leadership did not appreciate the idealism of the American President and his Fourteen Points. They had lost many men in the war and had seen the worst of military destruction in their homelands. Moreover, Wilson had decided to go to Paris to attend the peace conference at Versailles, which was also not appreciated by the Europeans. A President ranks above the Prime Ministerial level; they thought his presence was contrary to diplomatic protocol and would make negotiations more difficult. During the Peace Conference, Clemenceau was the victim of an assassination attempt and was severely wounded. He recovered, but that put him in a mood to demand heavy reparations from the Germans in the Treaty of Versailles.[8] The British felt the same way, so that in the final compromises between the Europeans and Wilson, they resolved their differences. France got the Saar region and Wilson got his League of Nations.[9]

The United States held its biennial election for Congress in 1918, in November shortly before the armistice was declared on November 11. The Republican Party won a majority of the seats in the House of Representatives and gained a majority in the Senate. All committee chairmanships therefore were held by Republicans, and that strengthened the hand of Senator Henry Cabot Lodge of Massachusetts, chairman of the Foreign Relations Committee which would ultimately reject the Treaty of Versailles. Lodge delayed for months committee consideration of the bill, and a motion to send it to the floor of the Senate.[10] Wilson had hoped for a vote during the Fall of 1919, but delay was in control in the Senate. Wilson decided to take the matter to the American people by traveling to various cities around the country to talk to them. In Pueblo, Colorado, he suffered a major stroke in the middle of a speech. He was brought back to Washington immediately by train.

Woodrow Wilson spent himself in his effort to get public support for the League. Throughout his life, going back to his university years, he worked with intensity. On the way he had several serious illnesses. In 1880-81 he had a stomach ailment while at law school. In 1895-96 he was near collapse and had a small stroke, with phlebitis in one leg. This stroke also made his right arm and hand useless. In 1906 he had a severe stroke, when a blood vessel burst in one eye. He and his wife Ellen went to England for three months, and at the end of that stay he had almost completely recovered. The final stroke in 1919 was the one he sustained in Colorado on the western trip to persuade the people to support the League of Nations. He survived this devastating attack, was actually able to walk when he was brought back to the White House, but he was not able to fully resume his role as President thereafter.[11] His second wife, Edith, who was able to communicate with him, handled the affairs of state for him following his direction, and his various advisors assisted in whatever way they could. He lived beyond the election of Warren Harding in 1920 and his inauguration in 1921. The Wilsons moved to a house on S Street in Washington where they lived until his death in1924.

THE PROGRESSIVES

The Progressive Party was formally constituted on August 6, 1912 when the party nominated Theodore Roosevelt for President. The party had already approved its platform as its expression of social justice: it advocated a minimum wage for women, the prohibition of child labor, workmen's compensation, and some form of social insurance. Moreover, the Progressives sought to democratize the electoral process. They advocated the initiative, referendum and recall for the States in order to give the public the means to initiate legislation and provide for referenda to enact it. The recall was intended to allow the public to get rid of public officials at the State level who were deemed corrupt or performing in ways that were harmful to society. In addition, they wanted a means to recall judicial decisions, perhaps the least successful item in their program. They advocated the nation-wide presidential primary. Furthermore, they urged the creation of a federal trade commission to exercise authority over businesses and a tariff commission to set tariff rates "on a scientific basis."[1] T.R.'s acceptance speech to the Bull Moose Convention which nominated him for President, "A Confession of Faith," gave his exhilarated audience what they wanted to hear: his social and economic program for reform based on its platform. He picked up almost all of the platform planks and spelled out their meaning for American society. The primary weight of his message was on the economy: business, industry, and labor and the economic effects that the great corporations have upon the working man. He talked of the unfair distribution of wealth in a rich country where, with some government regulation, everyone should be able to make a living, provide for families and children, and contribute to the general welfare. Roosevelt talked about the inadequate protection of people who worked in dangerous places like mines or in industries like steel. He urged standards of sanitation and safety, and compensation for work-related injury or death. Only government, State or federal, could protect people. And only the national government, as the "collective power of our people," could regulate the trusts.

He urged minimum wages, government established, and maximum hours for work. And he stressed the fundamental role of the farmer in the American economy. Government must cooperate with the farmer to make the farm more productive. He said over and over again that the existing condition of the economy was "abnormal."

"Wages are subnormal if they fail to provide a living for those who devote their time and energy to industrial occupations."

"Hours are excessive if they fail to afford the worker sufficient time to recuperate and return to his work thoroughly refreshed."

"(N)ight labor of women and children is abnormal and should be prohibited"

(T)he seven-day working week is abnormal, and we hold that one day of rest in seven should be provided by law.

We hold that the continuous industries, operating twenty-four hours out of twenty-four, are abnormal and should by law be divided into three shifts of eight hours.

Safety conditions are abnormal when, through unguarded machinery, poisons, electrical voltage, or otherwise, the workers are subjected to unnecessary hazards of life and limb. . .

Home life is abnormal when tenement manufacture is carried on in the household.

The premature employment of children is abnormal and should be prohibited. It is abnormal for any industry to throw back upon the community the human wreckage due to its wear and tear, and the hazards of sickness, accident, invalidism, involuntary unemployment and old age should be provided for through insurance. What Germany has done in the way of old-age pensions or insurance should be studied by us. . .

Working women have the same need to combine for protection that working men have...we do not believe that with the two sexes, there is identity of function; but we do believe that there should be equality of right; and therefore we favor woman suffrage.[2]

Thus Theodore Roosevelt, the Progressive Party candidate, labeled as "abnormal" the practices in industrial America that needed to be reformed. In this way he could disarm arguments like "this is the way we've always done it" and "it works all right, there's no need to change it." To be an "abnormal" nation would offend many people.

Woodrow Wilson could be equally passionate about the issues he raised in his two inaugural addresses and speeches he gave around the country. Wilson's New Freedom was a vision of everyone fulfilling his economic mission in the country with a minimum of government interference. For small business he thought in terms of economic freedom. The greatest threat to the small businessman was monopoly. Wilson took his economics from the attorney Louis Brandeis whom he had met in 1912 and found to be probative on the subject and sympathetic to Wilson's own outlook. Both believed government should intervene to preserve competition. He was convinced that when competition is allowed to work its way in the American economy, all elements in the economy, industry, workers, and farmers benefit. People will be best off if they manage their own lives and jobs. What needed to be done to preserve competitiveness was to try to prevent monopoly, regulate the trusts, provide agencies like the Federal Trade Commission to hear cases of unfair practices, particularly by the great corporations, and resolve them with a view to strengthening competition.

What is interesting about Wilson's economic views, and Brandeis', was that they believed there is a theory that can be applied to the relationships between government and the players in the economy. Wilson was a Jeffersonian Democrat. Brandeis may have classified his thinking that way too, but often in the 20th Century, a theory has been designed to apply to a particular constellation of forces at work in the society. Then it develops that the theory is only partially applicable to a situation, or only serves society for a time or only benefits one sector of the economy at a given time. The lesson of 20th Century American history seems to suggest that no one theory is applicable to the economy all of the time. Looking for an over-arching explanation of a problem in the economy and then designing a theory to deal with it is what Adam Smith did in his *An Inquiry Into the Nature and Causes of the Wealth of Nations*, where he was trying to describe what certain European nations were doing to cause them to prosper and what others were doing that caused them not to prosper. He found that entrepreneurs who were free to pursue their enterprises with little interference from government enhanced their own profit and that of the country. But this freedom was competitive, and that is what Smith saw as the key to a healthy economy. Wilson and Brandeis saw that unfettered competition would lead to monopoly unless government acted to balance competing interests.

Similarly, in 19th Century Europe, Karl Marx looked for broad theories of the relationships between capital and labor, found that labor was grossly exploited, and that the capitalist class would always exploit labor because government, inevitably pro-capital, would not want to intervene.[3] So, eventually, a revolution would occur, a revolt of the proletariat, to be followed for a time with a dictatorship of the proletariat. When social stability could be restored, the government would "wither away." Everyone would be free and equal.

The Progressive Party did not argue for a theory about labor and capital, or even a theory about competition in business except in the most practical manner. Unlike the Socialists, strong in Great Britain at this time, and unlike the Communists, pressing to apply their theory to Russia, the Progressive movement in the United States argued for specific reforms to advance practical ends. It was a reform movement, not a panacea. The platform the Progressive Party approved at its 1912 Convention later became the agenda of the Democratic Party in the 1930s.

Woodrow Wilson and Theodore Roosevelt differed in their prescriptions as to what should be done by government in the economy, but they were both progressives, both reformers. Wilson's New Freedom focused on freeing the businessman from the competitive pressures of monopolies while Roosevelt looked for ways to restrain the trusts while recognizing the ability of big businesses to produce more for the material benefit of the nation if let alone by government. His pragmatic program was intended to help the working man and woman, and establish a just system for all to work: the minimum wage, limits on hours of work required, prevention of child labor, safety requirements for workplaces, equal treatment of women on the job, and women's suffrage. He was not strong on States' rights because he was sure that the trusts always looked for such rights in courts of law. He was convinced that the only way to govern the trusts was through federal law. Meanwhile, Wilson opposed federal legislation which seemed to support workers or farmers or other actors in the economy as a form of special privilege. That was not competitive free enterprise in Wilson's view.

The Progressives of the early 20th Century defined politics in America for several decades. Franklin Roosevelt, taking office in 1933, sought legislation to advance the program of his illustrious fifth cousin whom FDR revered. Burdened by the Great Depression, with its 25% unemployment condition and the apparent resistance of the Supreme Court to rule against big business, Roosevelt fought for legislation to deal with the condition of the laboring man, the farmer's need for a living income, fair labor standards and the right of workers to form unions to bargain collectively with business. It was a pragmatic approach to dealing with the distressed economy and it reflected the Progressive movement's acceptance by a large segment of American society.

WARREN G. HARDING
1921-1923

President Harding wanted to restore the United States to what he called normalcy, and on this platform he and Calvin Coolidge, running for Vice-President, won the election of 1920 in a landslide, with 60% of the popular vote. The Democratic candidates seeking the nomination of their party were Ohio Governor James M. Cox and former Assistant Secretary of the Navy Franklin D. Roosevelt. Harding had served in the Senate from 1914, and became known for his good speaking voice. As a publisher, he knew the uses of language, and had made a name for himself by giving the nominating speech for Taft for President at the Republican National Convention in 1912. Although some important Republicans supporting him for President assured voters that he would advance the movement for membership in the League of Nations, Harding interpreted his election to be a mandate to stay out of the League.

American society in 1920 had not fully recovered from the settlements of the First World War. Whether to join the League of Nations continued to be an issue that divided the people. Cox and Roosevelt were passionate about joining, but important members of the Senate continued to oppose it, notably Henry Cabot Lodge.

Beyond this issue, the country was in a recession by 1920, as often happens immediately after a war. Furthermore, there were social disturbances like the race riot that occurred in Chicago in

1919 which President Wilson had tried to stop with conciliation and legislation. The riot was instigated by a predatory group of white youths, members of a sports club, who were looking for an opportunity. There were riots in other cities as well, in Tulsa, Oklahoma, for example. The root cause of the rioting was the large influx of thousands of blacks from the South during the war who were looking for jobs and homes in the cities, and there was insufficient space for them and there were insufficient job opportunities.

Warren Harding said, even before his nomination,

"America's present need is not heroics, but healing; not nostrums, but normalcy; not revolution, but restoration; not agitation, but adjustment; not surgery but serenity; not the dramatic, but the dispassionate; not experiment, but equipoise; not submergence in internationality, but sustainment in triumphant nationality..." [1]

Thus he would do nothing to try to bring peace to the rioting in some of the cities. Society would resolve any problems without federal government interference. He was confident that any problems in the economy would resolve themselves if let alone.

Foreign Policy

Republican foreign policy during the 1920s can be described as "involvement without commitment," as a historian of American foreign policy has explained. The '20s were not really a time of American retreat into isolationism though that decade is often so described.[2] As George C. Herring points out, Europe was exhausted from the Great War when some 60 million people were lost to war or war-related activities. The United States and Japan were the only nations that gained from the War. The U.S. was a creditor nation, the largest agricultural and manufacturing country in the world. It had an army of 140,000, adequate to the needs of the country at that time.[3] It also had the world's largest navy. With the potential of air power after the flight of Charles Lindbergh from New York to Paris, and America's posture of peace, the country's influence was felt everywhere. In short, the nation's power was apparent even though the world continued to think of Europe as the center of power. American culture spread to Europe in art, music and motion pictures. Part of this was, of course, American corporate culture.

The Secretary of State, Charles Evans Hughes, who ran unsuccessfully for President in 1916, served the country ably under the Harding and Coolidge Administrations. He led the Senate to approve some 71 treaties with other countries, all intended to benefit the United States in trading relationships.[4] After Hughes' years of service, Frank B. Kellogg, who had served as ambassador to Britain, was appointed to the post of Secretary of State. He is best remembered as the American negotiator of the Kellogg-Briand Pact of 1928. It was originally initiated by Foreign Minister Briand of France who intended it to be a bilateral agreement with the U.S., but under the aegis of Kellogg and President Coolidge, it was enlarged to become a 15-nation pact outlawing war as an instrument of national policy.[5] All of this was in keeping with the tenor of the times in the United States.

Warren Harding's term in office was short. He had allowed some of his friends from Ohio to use their offices in government to enrich themselves, and then he became very anxious about the possibility of scandal. Albert Fall, the Secretary of the Interior, granted some leases of federal land with oil reserves in Wyoming and California to men in the oil business. While the leasing was legal, what was not legal was the large financial gifts he received from those oil magnates who benefited from the leases. The publicity arising from the investigation of these actions greatly disturbed the President. Harding talked to his Secretary of Commerce, Herbert Hoover, asking him what he should do about it. Hoover urged him to address the scandal publicly and thus dispose of it by honestly reporting it and saying he rejected that kind of behavior in government.[6] Harding, having made his career in publishing back in Marion, Ohio, feared how the public would react to this. In the long run, however, the President did not have to cope with the matter; his heart condition became acute and he died in an attack in San Francisco in August, 1923.

President Harding and Vice-President Coolidge with their wives, 1921?
Library of Congress, Author: National Photo Company PD-US

JOHN CALVIN COOLIDGE
1923-1929

Vice-President Coolidge was informed of the death of the President while vacationing in Vermont. He got the word in the middle of the night, and arranged to take the oath of office before dawn on August 3, 1923. It was administered with his hand on the family Bible in the light of a kerosene lamp by his father, a notary public. The new President confronted the challenge of "restoring the dignity and prestige of the Presidency when it had reached the lowest ebb in our history. . .in a time of extravagance and waste. . ." in the words of Alfred Smith, a later Democratic candidate for President.[1]

Coolidge grew up the son of a village storekeeper in Plymouth, Vermont. He graduated with honors from Amherst College, and moved on to a career in law and politics in Northampton, Massachusetts. As President, he became popular for his outspoken isolationism in international politics and his laissez faire approach to the American economy. He perceived that the country was enjoying prosperity in 1924, and when he was re-elected with more than 54% of the popular vote, he said in his Inaugural Address, the United States had reached "a state of contentment seldom before seen."[2]

President Coolidge was known as "silent Cal" for his reluctance to respond to questions in interviews or at other times when he did not want to express his views. Walter Lippmann said of him in

1926, "The active inactivity suits the mood and certain of the needs of the country admirably. It suits all the business interests which want to be let alone. . . And it suits all those who have become convinced that government in this country had become dangerously complicated and top-heavy. . ."[3] This assessment did not reflect the importance of the business-government relationship which steered policy, both foreign and domestic, in the '20s. There was a large expansion of investments by American industry in foreign countries. This included not only Europe and the Middle East but notably Latin American countries.

The country was prosperous for some important elements in the economy. However, the President refused to use Federal authority to help agriculture, which was depressed, and he vetoed farm relief bills passed by the Congress. The idea of a Tennessee Valley Authority had been proposed in Congress, a plan that was later encouraged by Franklin Roosevelt and was adopted. The plan was to produce cheap electric power on the Tennessee River by a Federal agency. Coolidge opposed it; he was Puritan in his reluctance to spend Federal money.

The1920s were years when the National Association for the Advancement of Colored People was taking its issues to the public and to the courts. They pushed for anti-lynching legislation. The organization was strengthened by its early leaders like W.E.B. DuBois, a Harvard educator, and Ida B. Wells. There were others, but it is interesting that the Presidents of the NAACP were white men until 1975, although the executive directors were black. This probably was done to legitimize the organization in the minds of whites, some of whom were active contributors to the organization. Some of these contributors were Jews who sympathized with the blacks in racist America. For example, Julius Rosenwald who headed Sears Roebuck at one time, was generous in funding schools for black children in the South. The Presidents of the United States, however, were not active in leading the country away from racism during these years.

While vacationing in 1927, Calvin Coolidge announced that he did not wish to run for President again in 1928. Various reasons were understood to be responsible for his decision. One was that his 14-year-old son died of blood poisoning, and the President was depressed. He could not think about another term. Another was that his health was not good: he had chronic indigestion and needed more sleep than he was getting. Coolidge died in 1933.

HERBERT CLARK HOOVER
1929-1933

President Herbert Hoover wanted to lead the United States into a more enlightened economy and society using policies urged by the Progressive Republicans of a decade earlier and new understandings about organizations. In addition he brought to the office his own remarkable energy and his Quaker views of morality in the life of the individual and in the life of a society. His professional training was in engineering and geology, and he combined those skills with an aptitude for organization. He applied his broad learning and his experiences traveling as a scientist in Australia and China and his work providing humanitarian assistance in Europe during the First World War to his understanding of organization to produce new ways of doing things in the American government. He also had specific preparation for the job of President having served as Secretary of Commerce in the Harding and Coolidge Administrations. In this office he reorganized his Department into three bureaus: those concerning the Census, the Standards, and Foreign and Domestic Trade.

Hoover served in the Wilson Administration during and at the end of the First World War. He organized rescue services for the wounded and for refugees from war zones. During the war, he organized a major food distribution program for war-ravaged Europe, coordinating the work through the Committee for the

Relief of Belgium. After the War, Wilson appointed him to head up a food program distributing American agricultural products to devastated areas in Europe.

Herbert Hoover European Relief
Courtesy: Library of Congress

By this time he had some clearly developed policy ideas for what America should do to heal and rescue countries in Europe from the wreckage of war. He believed strongly in the League of Nations. In politics he had been a Democrat for Wilson, but by 1920 he knew the Democrats would not win the Presidency, and his heart was with the Progressive Republicans of the Theodore Roosevelt tradition. He, along with Republicans in Congress, urged the Republican candidate for President, Harding, to support the League of Nations. Harding appeared to be favorable, but after the election, he did not pursue it, believing that the American people did not want to be involved in the international body. He did appoint Hoover to his

Cabinet as Secretary of Commerce, for by this time Herbert Hoover had achieved prestige for his good work in Europe, and had been a successful businessman for some years as an engineer. Through his travels to and work in Australia and elsewhere he had amassed a fortune which supported him and his family, Lou and his two sons, and allowed him to make gifts of significant size to Stanford.

The Economy

Hoover's theories about American government and its role in the economy emphasized help by the government together with voluntarism by the many actors in the economy. So, he believed that government must provide some protections to the laboring man and these would take the form of regulations, but they should be based on consultations among those concerned. Hoover was a great believer in bringing people to conferences in Washington to work out through cooperative endeavor whatever problems existed in their sector of the economy. Basically, he trusted the competitive together with the cooperative nature of man. He had seen much of the cooperative motives of people in wartime Europe. He thought that self-interest and altruism can go together. Most particularly, he believed in education to solve many misunderstandings

As President, Hoover had a view of foreign relations that prevailed in much of the Twentieth Century. He saw trade with other countries as a benefit to all parties but he also did not want to see the United States reach a point of dependence on some one or another product or country. There must be national self-sufficiency, and the United States should not depend on investments by others for its economic health. He supported tariffs to protect American businesses. He pressed for disarmament, believing that nations should be relieved of the costs of military preparation. He believed the United States should join the League of Nations; the Senate saw otherwise and never approved membership of the international organization. Hoover also supported membership of this country in the World Court, and urged the Senate to adopt legislation for that purpose but that body did not bring the bill to a vote.[1]

While still a child, Bertie Hoover lost both his father (in 1880) and his mother (in 1884) from illnesses He was raised by distant relatives, lived in several different places: West Branch, Iowa, then Oregon and California. He was educated in a Quaker school and also in a Catholic school in these several cities where he lived. He did well in mathematics but otherwise had to learn and work on English usages. His language was crude until he could master it. He went to Stanford University, where the president of the University took an interest in him and was an important influence on his education. He majored in geology and engineering. He met Lou, his future wife, also a geology student, at Stanford. After graduating from the University, he got a job working on engineering projects in Australia and China. In this work, he gained experience in organizing and managing projects.[2]

Hoover's philosophy was not the Republican stereotype. Not only did he think that international organization was essential to promote peace, but he also believed in individualism and cooperation as the proper stance for the American citizen. He agreed with Adam Smith that individuals strive to achieve income and position and they thrive in competition with others, but he considered that posture to be properly governed by individual self-control and a disposition to cooperate with others to reach social goals.[3] His own experience convinced him that an individual can prosper through hard work and competing with others. His experience in war-devastated Europe convinced him that cooperation with others, helping those who needed it to help themselves, was vital to society. He felt that society as a whole could prosper if everyone would follow that pattern of living. The viewpoint was Quaker-like, though after his childhood he did not regularly attend Quaker meetings. His lifestyle, however, was patterned by the Quaker teaching of modesty, simplicity in dress and behavior, honesty and directness in dealing with others.

Hoover thought the Department of Commerce was designed to guide and protect the American economy. As Secretary, he promoted economic development by reorganizing the Department of numerous technical offices and agencies into a unified whole of 1600 employees, each with a mission. The bureaus of Census, Standards, and Foreign and Domestic Commerce carried out policy. Hoover, like many other modern administrators of the time, was impressed with the value of Frederick Taylor's "scientific management" philosophy. This approach to organization became important not only in private business but also in government at all levels. It called for nonpartisan management with expertise at several levels of organization but governed by policy-makers. He wrote on one occasion, "There is somewhere to be found a plan of individualism and associational activities that will preserve the initiative, the inventiveness, the individuality, the character of men and yet will enable us to synchronize socially and economically this gigantic machine that we have built out of applied science."[4]

One of Hoover's aspirations was to virtually eliminate poverty in the United States. He worried about the 1920-22 depression which, fortunately, was short-lived. As Secretary of Commerce, he urged businesses to not cut wages while he pressed government agencies to invest in public works projects, notably road building. By 1922, employment figures went up and it appeared that the American economy would restore its balance.

Herbert Hoover took the oath of office in March, 1929; in October, the first harbinger of the economic trouble to come was the stock market crash. For three and one-half years, the President struggled with the fallout using the tools of government to provide public works, stimulate the vehicles of finance, and to encourage wise investment while discouraging speculation. He proposed legislation to help regulate the stock market, such as the Securities and Exchange Commission. However, Congress did not pass the law until 1934 when Franklin Roosevelt recommended it. In November, Hoover started a series of conferences in the White House bringing business, labor, and agriculture representatives.

Hoover predicted a long period of hardship. He thought that people without jobs would number 2 to 3 million. He urged cooperation to prevent "liquidation" of labor.[5] Hoover moved to stimulate employment and got voluntary pledges from business leaders. He increased public works and other construction spending. Businesses and labor cooperated, businesses by increasing investment and labor by withdrawing its latest wage demands. Henry Ford increased wages and cut prices. Hoover asked all State Governors to speed up public works projects within their States. He asked Congress to double the resources for public buildings and dams, highways, harbors, and a tax cut and a lowering of the federal discount rate by the Federal Reserve Board.

The President proposed legislation for an old age pension for all Americans over 65. He would pay them $50 a month.[6]. He proposed to Congress a farm program and bill. The Smoot-Hawley tariff was passed by Congress but not with the modest reforms Hoover proposed in 1930. It raised import duties by up to 100% -- this was harmful to consumers and set up a wall of import duties that would discourage foreign trade. The President signed it, but this was a bad time to shut out foreign goods because it prevented cheaper goods from coming into the country.[7] Hoover had a group of proposals to offer to Congress in Dec. 1929: a Federal Power Commission, federal subsidies for county health units, a rural child health program, reform of railroad rates and the banking system, new prisons and the extension of Civil Service protection for tri-level postmasters. He set up an Emergency Committee for Employment which organized 3,000 chapters around the country using publicity to sell the idea that it was a good time for home building.

Hoover provided much substance for the later New Deal, but he could not persuade the public or Congress to support all of his proposals. For example, he proposed a Securities and Exchange Commission designed to regulate the stock market but this was not passed until the year after he left office. Hoover spoke his mind, and was often blunt, part of his Quaker heritage. Unlike Franklin Roosevelt, he was not a salesman of proposals and ideas. However, he always made it clear where he stood with people of all stations in life. He could be very kind.

There was much public praise for the President's intervention in 1929-30. Newspapers said "no one could have done more", and in the past, Van Buren, Cleveland, and T.R. had not done as much. His "cool and superlative leadership" was praised. When he learned that employment was on the rise, he thought and told people that the economic crisis would end in the spring.[8]

But things were not better and the economy was not as advertised. Five percent of the population controlled one-third of the nation's wealth.[9] The average worker in 1929 had an income of less than $1500. Wages did not keep pace with the great productivity of the decade. There were 26 million new cars, consumer goods were flooding the market, production was overextended. So consumer debt grew; while it could be carried in prosperous times, it was huge burden in a recession and depression. Workers did not get higher wages or shorter hours with improvements in technology. With some level of unemployment throughout the 1920s, there was less buying power.

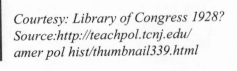

Courtesy: Library of Congress 1928?
Source:http://teachpol.tcnj.edu/
amer pol hist/thumbnail339.html

"American prosperity was largely bogus, limited to the 5 percent of the pop that controlled at least 1/3 of nation's wealth,"[10] as one biographer explained. The great technological achievements of the U.S. made many observers think that recovery was on the way, because the material aspects of the nation were growing so rapidly. But when things did not get better, Hoover called for voluntary cooperation by business and labor, and used optimistic statements and publicity to restore some confidence.[11]

Secretary of the Treasury Andrew Mellon's policy of tax reduction increased funds available for speculation. Lower rates for capital gains taxes took investors out of municipal bonds and into stocks.[12] There is more risk, of course, with investing in stocks. Hoover said on one occasion, "The only trouble with capitalism is capitalists. They're too damned greedy."[13]

Hoover could not see that this was not merely a credit crisis following upon a stock market crash and the fears of bankers. It involved jobs, contracts, relief money, pensions, elements that fluctuate. Hoover thought that the fundamentals of the economy were sound.

As if problems in the economy were not enough, there was a severe drought in the Great Plains in August, 1930. It drained money from Hoover's Farm Board which had been set up to give money to farmers for their crops. Earlier, when he formed the Federal Farm Board, he said to its members,

> I know there is not a thinking farmer who does not realize that all this cannot be accomplished by a magic wand or an overnight action. Real institutions are not built that way. If we are to succeed it will be by strengthening the foundations and the initiative which we already have in farm organizations, and building steadily upon them with the constant thought that we are building not for the present only but for the next year and the next decade.[14]

The President advanced the idea of price supports for farm products by buying surplus crops outright. But price supports were not adopted for some years because the idea was slow to be accepted. Hoover advocated government loans to cooperatives and also called for a Tennessee Valley Authority to be planned by his Bureau of Reclamation. Similar work was needed in central California as well.[15] The TVA became a reality only in the Roosevelt Administration.

One biographer observed that the government focused on reviving finance, in the belief that industrial recovery would follow, rather than dealing directly with unemployment and too low prices, and overproduction by farmers. It is ironic that Franklin Roosevelt and perhaps many in Congress had the same perceptions as Hoover about what was needed for the economy to revive. Not until 1939 was public works spending raised significantly.[16]

Underlining this view, the Reconstruction Finance Corporation grew out of Hoover's and Andrew Mellon's National Credit Finance Corporation. In a harbinger of the crash of 2008, Congress and the public, resented his (Hoover's) apparent eagerness to loan RFC funds by the tens of millions to hobbled financial institutions while dismissing individual relief as an insult to American character. They forgot that he asked Congress to adopt a Public Works Administration in his December 1931 message, only to see the proposal languish on the vine until FDR revived it and made the PWA his own, or that his angry call for a Senate investigation of unethical stock market practices paved the way for Roosevelt's Securities and Exchange Commission.[17]

The President made a point of eliminating the privileges of government officials, beginning with himself. He retired the presidential yacht and closed the White House stables. Not only that, when the Depression became worse, Hoover turned back to the government some of his salary.

While Hoover was a facts and figures man, preferring rational discussion to emotional responses to problems, he also clearly fulfilled the Quaker values he had learned as a child. He was much concerned for racial justice, and made a point of giving encouragement to black leaders in voluntary organizations and in the academic arena. Biographers also note that he sought prison reform, and was concerned about the condition of American Indians, all policies supported by Quakers. Hoover also believed that Prohibition was wrong because it was unenforceable. He himself enjoyed a cocktail at night, and wine with his dinner.

President Hoover was convinced that the public should be concerned about the condition of children in the United States. He invited some 2500 delegates from voluntary and social welfare agencies, including some from local, state and federal governments to a conference in the White House to deal with child welfare. A very long report of 35 volumes came out of that conference and was used by agencies for decades. Hoover supported the idea of a new Department of Education.[18]

Hoover campaigned vigorously for re-election in 1932 but lost to Franklin Roosevelt. He was angry about this because he thought Roosevelt's charges against him in the election campaign were not only unfair but untrue. The Depression was upon the nation. Hoover had done his best to resolve the economic distress, but the blame game was in full cry. Hoover became a scapegoat for the hard times of the Great Depression.

Foreign Policy

In foreign affairs, the President and Prime Minister Ramsey Macdonald of Britain agreed to hold a naval disarmament conference. It was held in Washington in 1930 with Britain and Japan attending, and the three agreed to reduce their armaments to a 5-5-3 ratio of naval strength.[19]

In Europe, the Depression brought problems similar to those the United States had suffered. Germany's banking system collapsed.

France declined to participate in Hoover's move to suspend debt payments by Germany to the European powers as well as to the United States. What followed in due course was the selection of Adolph Hitler by President Paul von Hindenburg in Germany to be chancellor, and the election of a new government in Britain which took that country off the gold standard. This had a harmful effect on the United States because it allowed gold to flow out of the country. Meanwhile, in the Far East, Japan invaded Manchuria.

Hoover's foreign policy came out of his experiences in other countries. Henry Stimson, his Secretary of State, "expressed astonishment at the new president's grasp of foreign policy." He knew more about the world than most diplomats, Stimson said.[20] His travels as an engineer and geologist and his humanitarian work in Europe during and after the war contributed much to his sophistication about other countries.

Hoover rejected the idea of war whatever the circumstance. In 1932, "The League of Nations adopted (the President's) tactics of moral pressure in lieu of economic quarantine." This concerned Japan's building up of its military forces. Stimson thought this had the seeds of future conflict. When Japan invaded Manchuria, Hoover called "for the civilized nations of the world to withhold recognition of any territory gained through aggression."[21]

Hoover mediated a border dispute between Chile and Peru, and he negotiated treaties of arbitration or conciliation with 42 countries. He withdrew U.S. troops from Haiti and Nicaragua and pledged "noninterference in the internal affairs of Latin America."[22]

Quakers had taken a strong position for the use of a World Court to provide a means for arbitration or conciliation of disagreements among nations at the two Hague conferences held in the early years of the Twentieth Century. The President's use of his own good offices was also a vehicle for resolving differences among nations and it was characteristic of Quaker policy.

Domestic Policy

Hoover was a whirlwind of activity for reforms in a large variety of contexts. The economic context came to be the hardest issue when the economy would not respond to his efforts to correct the markets. But there were others. He saw to it that a number of jobs in the White House were filled by Negroes, and raised the number of blacks in all federal employment to 54,684 by the end of 1932. He enlisted the Julius Rosenwald fund to support a conference on the Economic Status of the Negro. He had long advocated a means of providing land to Negroes so that they could own it, farm it and make a living for themselves. Tenants and sharecroppers would benefit, whatever their race, but this effort bore little fruit. He invited Negroes, notably President Moton of Tuskegee Institute, to the White House to discuss his plan with financiers. Hoover's motive was to help Negroes help themselves but he was not an integrationist. And his administration purged blacks from the Republican Party in the South, ostensibly to get rid of corrupt leaders.[23] However, Hoover believed in racial justice and defended civil liberties to the point of ordering the Attorney General to investigate the methods used by police in the District of Columbia.

By any measure, Herbert Hoover was a very good President of the United States. He coped as well as he could given the understandings of the American people and the economic system of his time. It was a great injustice that he was associated with the Depression for a generation after he served. Roosevelt and the New Deal got much credit for imaginative and forward-looking proposals for helping the nation out of the Depression, but many of those ideas were Hoover's. Such is the nature of a democracy, where the people have to explain why something has happened and who was responsible for it. At least it is heartening to read the work of scholars who were able to use original and some believed lost sources to tell the true story of Herbert Hoover, the President.

FRANKLIN DELANO ROOSEVELT
1933-1945

If Theodore Roosevelt coped with an industrializing society fraught with economic stresses and Woodrow Wilson had to decide whether to go to war, and how to manage it, Franklin Roosevelt had to confront both major stresses: an economy gone bad with the Great Depression and a 25% unemployment figure and, eight years later, attacks on American ships by the Japanese at Pearl Harbor and by German submarines in the Atlantic. It is true that FDR and Winston Churchill had both concluded that the Germans were a threat and that ultimately the Americans would have to help Britain fight the Germans, but the attack by the Japanese while their envoys were in Washington to discuss mutual interests was unexpected, and the damage to American shipping was huge. Essentially, the Pacific fleet of the United States was destroyed.

Franklin Roosevelt took the oath of office in 1933, well aware of the injustices in society and the severe impact of the Depression on low-income workers and their families. In his first inaugural address, the President, crippled by polio ten years earlier, urged people to not fear but to work and to come forward with ideas which would solve the serious situation.

The Economy

As Americans entered the 1930s, there was evidence all around the economy that unrestrained capitalism was not sound economic policy but many people did not know what to do about it. The "system" did not seem to work. Why wasn't free enterprise working in American industry as Adam Smith had theorized? Where was the belief in progress? What would the nation do with the unions? These were considered dangerous, threatening the stability of society. It almost looked as if Karl Marx was right: capitalism creates a poor working class whose job it was to produce goods and services at whatever wages and working conditions the captains of industry devised.

Bread line, New York City 1932, snprelief 1a
www.eyewitnesstohistory.com/snprelief1 htm 20k

In 1933, people were not interested in theories. Nor was Roosevelt. The new President and his advisers came to the conclusion that major interventions in the economy had to be undertaken to rescue the country from further distress. What they came up with was termed a New Deal. The government-supported programs they introduced were controversial from the beginning, but they did set a pattern which was gradually adopted by Congress and slowly began to succeed. The President approached the situation with pragmatic solutions. He was prepared to experiment, to improvise. If he had a philosophy, it was to move toward a middle way. No extremes of action. And he looked for ways to work with the people who were involved in a particular sector of the economy.

In the first hundred days, he and his "brain trust" produced a collection of measures to resolve specific problems. What to do about the banks closing when people could not get their money out. What to do about the agricultural crisis created by excessive amounts of corn and wheat produced but not sold. Farmers could not earn enough to pay on their mortgages or buy essential resources and equipment to continue to farm. Farm property also lost value in this situation. What about people out of work having no source of income? What about the condition of older people who had retired and lost their pensions in the Depression? What about the growing slums where people could not live in safety, not to mention in healthful conditions? Why did not the "free enterprise system" resolve the major issues so that there would not be so much poverty?

Dust storm approaching Stratford, Texas
Credit: NOAA George E. Marsh Album, April 18, 1935
Source: http://www.photolib.noaa.gov/historic/c&gs/theb1365.htm

The New Deal's policies were broadly applied to the spectrum of problems the country confronted in 1933. The Agricultural Adjustment Act was one of the first of the new administration. Its purpose was to restore prices for farm products to a relationship with non-agricultural prices that prevailed between 1909 and 1914. This relationship was called parity. To achieve this, there would be processing taxes which would equal the difference between actual prices and parity. Money would be realized which could pay for the reducing of farm production. Historically, American agriculture has produced more than was consumed. The problem was overproduction. So, in order to strengthen the prices that farmers would receive for their produce, specifically for certain crops, wheat, corn, cotton, tobacco, the AAA supported acreage restrictions on planting. Plant every third row, or kill every third pig, as the newspapers explained.[1] It was all designed to deal with the large capacity of American agriculture, the overproduction of which kept prices down. To provide the farmer with income, there would be government price supports for crops he could not realize by normal cultivation. This worked for the large commercial farmers who were represented in the groups that drafted the law under the leadership of Henry Wallace, the Secretary of Agriculture. But small farmers, of whom there were millions, were not consulted nor represented among Wallace's interest groups. The result was many small farmers who were very angry about this new law.[2] The early results of the AAA appeared to be positive, however; prices did advance. However, the Supreme Court struck down the AAA; the government then proposed a different way to accomplish that goal. It purchased amounts of produce and sold it abroad at depressed prices, meanwhile using price supports to bolster the income of the farmer.

Franklin Roosevelt could translate a situation into a solution that appealed to the positive side of people. The Works Progress Administration, which took up the idea of giving people jobs on public works projects like road building, originally one of Hoover's initiatives, was presented by Roosevelt as building for the future of America. It tied into people's aspirations and sense of community. It expressed his optimism.

Roosevelt thought that other measures the government had adopted would move the whole economy forward and this would help agriculture. The National Industrial Recovery Act, for example, was another early law adopted as part of the New Deal's effort to stimulate the economy. The idea was for business people themselves to draw up codes of fair competition which the President would review. If he approved them they would become law. There was to be a code for each industry.[3] The expectation was that the codes would reduce waste in the competition between industries, would bring about better prices and establish benefits labor had been seeking for a generation, higher wages, shorter hours and safer working conditions. This was the kind of voluntary self government that Hoover thought would promote economic benefit to all.

The self-government feature was to consist of agreements by industrial groups to be followed by the many businesses within a certain industry. Labor standards in wages and hours would be agreed to in such a code, as would the right of labor to bargain collectively. These codes would be exempt from antitrust laws, but those laws would remain applicable where industry codes had not been developed. A means of control by government would be set through licensing to keep businessmen following the requirements of the codes. Finally, in a separate section of the bill, money for a vast public works program was provided.

The NIRA provided recognition of the right of workers to organize and bargain collectively with industry. Again, as in agriculture, the President was working with interest groups and mediating among them. But there were groups vehemently opposed to the NIRA which had been designed to modify antitrust laws in order to prevent unfair competition. After much discussion and numerous proposals for this part of a recovery, the final compromise provided that there could be councils within an industry that could draw up the codes of fair competition to be approved by the President. The provisions for collective bargaining and for wage and hour standards were not clearly stated in the law. Ultimately, the Supreme Court struck down the NIRA as prescribing measures covering industry and labor that invaded the practices of normal free enterprise.

Recovery was the goal, of course, or at least visible signs of recovery. The economy responded with unbalanced ups and downs. Employment figures went up and down in 1933-34. Other measures were also erratic. Fortunately for the New Deal, but not as a result of any effort by the President,[4] who was thrown off his stride by the opposition, the Wagner Act was approved by Congress just before the Court struck down the NIRA. Senator Robert Wagner of New York had drafted the bill and gained the support of enough Senators that he could introduce his National Labor Relations bill. After much political effort by Wagner, the bill was passed by both Senate and House. The Wagner Act gave company unions the power to organize and bargain collectively with industry, which would not have been realized otherwise with the demise of the NIRA. Near the end of the legislative process, Roosevelt supported the bill.

The Supreme Court struck down the Agricultural Adjustment Act in 1936, and followed that action by striking down a New York minimum wage law. This Roosevelt, the former New York Governor, deplored. The Court in his opinion had created a "no man's land" where neither the national nor the state governments could function.[5]

A year later, though, the New Deal's legislative program moved forward. Congress passed the Fair Labor Standards Act of 1937 which essentially defended the position of unions by stating what were fair working standards: hours, pay, safety features in industry.[6] The Works Progress Administration gave many people jobs on public works construction projects. This was a response not only to the unemployment situation but also to the needs for public infrastructure improvements in the country. At this time also, Congress passed legislation creating several programs to help people who could not help themselves. Aid to Families with Dependent Children was first subsidized at this time. Old Age Assistance was instituted, and its later successor the Social Security program. Aid to the Blind was begun in these years, as was Aid to the Permanently and Totally Disabled.

The national Public Housing program was begun in 1937, with federal funding assistance and construction requirements for local Housing Authorities. This act was the product of lobbying by local housing organizations, particularly in Chicago and New York that appealed to the government for a law that would provide funds to help local public authorities build low-rent housing.

The President had several special projects he wanted to pursue. One was a civilian conservation corps intended to employ 250,000 young men in building dams, planting trees, and undertaking scores of conservation projects. One of these projects was to conserve parts of the Tennessee Valley and develop hydroelectric facilities. This was to be done through the creation of a public authority, a unit of government whose responsibility would be to raise money through fees or taxes, plan and build a dam and other facilities to provide electric power to the people who lived in the Tennessee Valley.

Politics in those years, and even in these years, often was defined as right vs left. The left in the '30s connoted socialism; for some even the kind of socialism called communism that people saw in the Soviet Union. The right connoted the free enterprise economy, laissez faire. Roosevelt's pragmatism made some people think his early policies were too far left: the Agricultural Adjustment Act, the National Industrial Recovery Act, the TVA, and the Civilian Conservation Corps. There was too much involvement of the government, they said. But FDR insisted that he was going right down the middle.

When the President had reached the limit of his patience with the Supreme Court by its decisions, he took counsel with his advisers and concluded that the best way to reduce the political impact of the Court's out-dated perceptions of the American economy and polity was simply to increase the number of Justices. If he couldn't beat them with logical argument, he could beat them with numbers. He would appoint lawyers and judges who saw the needs of the country as he did. But the public, which saw the Supreme Court as elevated above politics, as the protector of the Constitution, could not countenance tampering with that Court. Congress advised the President that he would not be successful with such a plan, it would not be supported by the legislators. A much weaker plan for reform of the Court was passed by the Congress, but only after a bitter fight which hurt all sides.[7] However, within a year or two, four of the Justices resigned and opened the way for new appointments. Roosevelt appointed mostly Democrats to fill the vacancies on the Court.

Recovery was sporadic in 1933-34; employment seemed to rise, and then unemployment numbers surpassed employment numbers. Government lending through the Reconstruction Finance Corporation came along with government spending through public works and benefits to farmers who agreed to plant only every third row. The Tennessee Valley was under development and provided a way to transform that area from being a drain on the economy to a stimulus to it. Putting money into people's hands in key areas of the economy did seem to be working to the benefit of the economy. The Wagner Act provided for the right of a labor organization in an industry to sit down with management and bargain for wages, hours and working conditions.

Because of the distress of the Depression and the subsequent recession in 1937-38, there seemed to be no way to bring about an economic recovery. Many people, some knowledgeable, some not, offered advice to the President. John Maynard Keynes, the Englishman who had written a treatise about his theory of economy, sent Roosevelt a letter telling him what was wrong with the New Deal's approach to the falling stock market, the increasing unemployment numbers and the crisis facing the financial sector. Keynes and Roosevelt had met once and liked each other, so this letter to the President was not out of line. But Keynes was recommending action that Roosevelt could not agree to. The Keynesian solution was massive government investment in the economy while lowering taxes. The result would be major deficit[8] spending with no balancing of the budget. While Roosevelt and the Congress decided to invest in a large spending program to strengthen the Works Progress Administration and provide money for infrastructure programs, he always promised to balance the budget when the current crisis was over. He believed in a balanced budget and could not accept the kind of program Keynes recommended.

A biographer explains the President's position by simply saying that Roosevelt did not understand economics and dismissed the theories of economists. Deficit financing as a normal practice was not practical and certainly not safe as a long-term solution to depressions and recessions in his mind.

> And now, by a supreme irony, fate placed before this man of practicality an economic theory that seemed to embody only uncommon sense. The idea of boosting spending and holding down taxes and of doing this year after year as a deliberate policy, the idea of gaining prosperity by the deliberate creation of huge debts—this idea in its full dimensions seemed but another fanciful academic theory, and Roosevelt by 1938 had had a bellyful of such theories.[9]

What really restored the economy was the Second World War with its huge government investment in defense industries.

War and Foreign Policy

The shock of the attack on Pearl Harbor at the end of 1941 and the loss of so many of the naval personnel and so much of the nation's fleet devastated the former Assistant Secretary of the Navy.

The war was an agony for Roosevelt. But with determination he asked Congress to declare war on Japan and Germany and he told the American people that new ships and tanks and weapons would be built. Since he had already given Churchill and the British the assurances that the United States would help them with the Lend-Lease program, which Congress had approved, there was already underway some degree of warlike preparation in the United States. After Pearl Harbor, a rushed construction program of the so-called Liberty ships was ordered. The draft called up a military force of millions of men for the Army, Navy, their respective air arms, Marine Corps and Coast Guard. Women too volunteered for military duty, and were put in non-combat jobs. Orders for all manner of the weapons of war went out to manufacturing plants. Automobile plants were converted to make war materiel. The United States had never seen such a huge mobilization of resources; it was raised to fight a two-front war, one in the Pacific and one in the Atlantic and in Europe.

President Roosevelt and Prime Minister Churchill
at Atlantic Charter Conference, 10-12 August, 1941
U.S. Naval Historical Center Photograph.

There had been a short history of conferences between the British, Russians and Americans about the War, about the best strategy to defeat the Germans and the Italians. Early on, there had been conferences between Roosevelt and Churchill in Newfoundland and in Washington. In 1943 at Casablanca, Roosevelt and Churchill agreed that the Americans should invade Sicily and Italy and should launch their attack from North Africa, where British troops had been fighting the desert war against German Field Marshal Rommel. The plan was to attack the "soft underbelly" of southern Europe and move northward. Then, a much-debated attack on the Germans in France and northern Europe would form a pincers movement, ultimately to bring a surrender from Germany. When to begin a second front in the north, however, was the main issue. German submarine warfare in the Atlantic made it difficult to plan a major American troop transfer to Britain from which an invasion could be launched. Continued American presence by sea and by air would be essential. At the end of Casablanca conference, Roosevelt stated that the policy of the Allies was the unconditional surrender of Germany.[10]

At the later conferences, the Big Three debated and argued over what to do about a defeated Germany, which condition they were dedicated to bringing about. Churchill agreed to a partition of Germany among the four powers, to include France. The Soviets wanted reparations in the form of human labor to rebuild Russia where the Germans had devastated cities in attacks. The Big Three talked about making Germany a pastoral state, one unable to wage war again. The Soviets wanted a dismemberment of Germany. Roosevelt suggested a decentralized Germany, presenting a map showing four sectors for the four powers to govern Germany.[11] Finally, this was accepted, but Stalin wanted spheres of influence over the countries of Eastern Europe. This became the Soviet satellite system of repression in Czechoslovakia, Hungary, Bulgaria, Yugoslavia, Albania, and Poland. Over the years after the war, once

Soviet control of East Germany was ended, the nation became unified and Germany became a prosperous federation with an important role in the European community. Meanwhile, Soviet control over its Eastern European satellites was also ended. The Soviet Union itself was dissolved as a communist nation and its composition became the nation of Russia, and the Commonwealth of Independent States. But in 1945 this denouement was decades in the future.

Many Americans loved Franklin Roosevelt and thought that he was the President of the century; others hated him. He had remarkable interpersonal skills, was persuasive to the point that some people on whom he exerted his considerable charm wondered how he had persuaded them. He was optimistic about the future of the country even in its darkest days of the war and his optimism was contagious. The war and Roosevelt's persuasive powers brought the country out of isolationism and into the prospect of international organization. Indeed, his Administration set the foreign policy agenda for the rest of the Century. He was forceful in mobilizing the nation for the war and was effective in dealing with the allied powers. His experience as Assistant Secretary of the Navy in the Wilson administration helped prepare him for the work of waging war. It was that experience also that convinced him the United States should join the League of Nations, and when that failed he did not forget it, but brought it back to create the kind of peace that Wilson had thought would prevent wars in the future. He and his Cabinet members, particularly Cordell Hull, fashioned a structure for the United Nations, collaborating with government leaders among the allied powers. Hull was later given the Nobel Peace Prize for his work of drawing up a plan for the United Nations, and he is called the "Father of the UN." [12]

Secretary of State Cordell Hull, served 1933-1944.
en.wikipedia.org/wiki/Cordell Hull 99k

As for the economy, Roosevelt was willing to experiment with solutions to the economic distress of the nation since there did not seem to be any clear direction the government should go. Some people resented his solutions because they did not fit the laissez-faire idea of the economy, but he was showing them that that idea would no longer suffice. He and his advisers and some members of Congress could see that the segments of the economy that were suffering had to be helped by the government; the old belief in social Darwinism was discredited. It did not die out entirely, however, and continues to turn up in political speeches of one kind or another.

Social Stresses

There were continuing social stresses, particularly racism, that Roosevelt may have hoped would be moderated to some degree by the wartime economy, when jobs would be available to those who were not absorbed in the military. His wife, Eleanor, was a major force for attacking racism, however. She resigned from the Daughters of the American Revolution in 1939 when that group denied the singer Marian Anderson the opportunity to sing at Constitution Hall in Washington. Eleanor Roosevelt arranged for the event to be held at the Lincoln Memorial on the Mall in the heart of the nation's capital. Ms Anderson thrilled the large crowd with her beautiful singing. This was not the only time when Mrs. Roosevelt took action in behalf of blacks; she visited them in hospitals when the casualties of the war brought them home. She came back after trips around the country to talk to the President about the needs of the poor, black or white. She was more conscious of the social and economic disparities in the country than he, and in fact he came to rely on her reports to him with her broadening knowledge about conditions in the United States after her travels.

Marian Anderson greeted by Harold L. Ickes, Secretary of Interior, at her concert at Lincoln Memorial. Curator of online exhibit: Nancy Shawcross, Univ. Of Penna.

Franklin's death within weeks of the surrender by Germany in 1945 was expected by many, but very few people, only his wife Eleanor and the doctors knew that he had had a serious heart condition, an enlarged heart, for some time. Having suffered polio as a forty-year old man, his physical condition was always a concern to his family and friends. He overcame his physical disability and it was this mental vigor, also seen in his cousin Theodore, that carried Franklin through the trials of handling the economic crisis and then the war. His own experience could have been the root of his impulse to say to the people of his nation in 1933, "we have nothing to fear but fear itself."

HARRY S. TRUMAN
1945-1953

Everyone in the White House, including Vice-President Truman, could see that the President was a sick man. Truman thought he could not survive another four years. When he returned from the Yalta conference in February, Roosevelt had dark circles under his eyes, had lost weight and his appearance was one of exhaustion. In an address to the House and Senate, he spoke from a sitting position instead of standing, his legs braced, as he usually did.

On April 12, 1945, Eleanor Roosevelt summoned Truman to the White House and told him that the President was dead. Truman took the oath of office that night at the White House and began to prepare himself for the huge tasks ahead. One of his first decisions was to order that the San Francisco conference to create a United Nations organization proceed on schedule in April, two weeks after the death of Franklin Roosevelt.

The contrast between the new President and the former could not have been more striking. Roosevelt the patrician, schooled in the urbane, sophisticated environment of the American East Coast and an Ivy Leaguer (Harvard), had traveled widely in Europe as a child. Harry Truman, the farmer and haberdasher from Independence, a suburb of Kansas City, Missouri, had never attended college because he needed to be home working on the farm. He enjoyed reading, though, and was self-taught; he knew American history and had learned the Constitution. He was an Army Captain in Europe during the First World War. Like Roosevelt, he was gregarious, he enjoyed people.

As he grew older, Truman found politics in the Jackson County Courthouse and became a beneficiary of the Pendergast "machine" in Kansas City. Tom Pendergast was not a politician, he was a businessman who owned the Ready Mix Concrete company. He made money and spread his influence by getting local government contracts for his concrete. In addition, he arranged patronage jobs in the county for hundreds of followers. Politics in that environment was a matter of exchanging favors, and Harry Truman learned early that one must keep his commitments. Pendergast helped Truman get elected Jackson County Presiding Judge, an administrative position that helped prepare the future President to govern. In time Truman ran for the U.S. Senate, won and from there he made his mark in national Democratic politics.

Of short stature, Truman was an active man, rather excitable; as one historian said of him, Truman was combative but folksy, and "peppery."[1] He applied himself to his job as President with great vigor even though at the beginning he felt awkward and alone. His wife Bess was his mainstay; they were devoted to each other. Harry Truman gave his all while in office, as he promised he would. After he had served two terms as President (he could have served a third, the 22nd Amendment had not yet taken effect), he went home to Independence and lived another 20 years.

Foreign Policy

Truman knew little about foreign affairs and at first was naïve with the likes of "Uncle Joe" Stalin, yet his administration of almost eight years sparkled with foreign policy achievements. His first job was to accept the "unconditional surrender" of Germany on May 8, 1945 and carry out the terms of Roosevelt's agreements with the Allies about the governance of Germany. The plan was that the country would be divided into four sectors, each occupied and governed by one of the allied powers, which included France. Berlin, well within the Soviet occupation zone, was similarly divided into four sectors. The three Western countries made the city a showcase for Western culture, while East Berlin suffered under harsh Soviet control and lack of money.

President Truman had the awesome responsibility to consider and decide whether to drop an atomic bomb on Japan in order to bring about the surrender of that country to the United States. He did not know until it was tested, of course, quite how awesome that weapon would be. It had enormous destructive power, worth about 20,000 tons of TNT. He said he intended to tell the Japanese about the new weapon and to warn them of its power, urging them to surrender, but the ultimatum he signed with Churchill and agreed to by Chiang Kai-Shek, the leader of the Chinese Nationalist regime, did not give details about this as an atomic weapon or that it had the destructive power of 20,000 tons of TNT. It did, however, stress the weapon's power and urged the Japanese government to surrender.[2] The President did consider how best to communicate with the Japanese government before sending the bomb-carrying plane but he was never in doubt that the weapon had to be used.

The Japanese government communicated with the Soviet government that it would be interested in a meeting with them. The American government speculated that perhaps the purpose was to negotiate to keep the Russians from entering the war, or perhaps to get support for trying negotiations with the U.S.[3] When the Big Three met in Potsdam, Stalin told Truman of this. Truman already knew it from intercepts the American government had obtained. Meanwhile, upon his arrival in Potsdam, he got word from Secretary of War Stimson that the test of an atomic device in New Mexico had revealed an explosion of enormous power. The development of an atomic weapon had been intended for use to end that war, and now it seemed that such an opportunity was within reach.

Earlier, before the war, scientists in a number of European countries were studying the possible uses of atomic energy: the United Kingdom, Germany, France, Italy and Denmark. Because of the war, the British decided to work in the United States with American scientists to find a military application for atomic power. Germany was working hard for such a weapon. The Soviet Union was interested in the subject as well, but the Soviets went about the matter differently. They had spies within the Manhattan project. When Truman decided to tell Josef Stalin at their Potsdam Conference that a device had been successfully tested in New Mexico, Stalin did not react as Truman expected; the President thought that he did not comprehend. Actually, as Truman learned later, the Soviets knew exactly what the Americans were doing during several years of the development of the project. In the years that followed the war, the names of the spies became known: Alan Nunn May, a British scientist and later Klaus Fuchs a British physicist. In addition, two American citizens serving as couriers between Fuchs and Los Alamos were linked to later spying on atomic energy projects, Julius and Ethel Rosenberg. They were tried for treason, convicted, and executed in 1953.

In the President's mind, and that of Stimson and the military leaders, were the memories of the unprovoked attack on Pearl Harbor, and the savage treatment of prisoners. They remembered the infamous Bataan death march when American and Filipino prisoners were forced to march 80 miles in 4 days without food or water, and the Japanese shot stragglers, or stabbed them with bayonets.[4] The treatment of American prisoners in prison camps was barbaric. A final consideration in the minds of the Americans was the high cost of an invasion of the Japanese homeland. The experiences of the American invasions of Okinawa and Iwo Jima, the large losses of life and the kamikaze (suicide) attacks on American shipping in the Pacific near the end of the war were additional considerations. How many more of our military forces would be lost in an invasion? Japanese civilians as well as military forces would also be lost.

With the comfort of armchair hindsight, many people in the United States as elsewhere in the world today think that the U.S. should have staged a demonstration of the bomb's destructive power before Japanese leaders somewhere over the Pacific. That would be to presuppose a peaceful environment, not the frenzied maelstrom of war in the Pacific. Given the Japanese disposition at the time, would they have come to such a demonstration? Their disposition was to fight to the last man. The American military thought that they were fanatic. Surrender was unthinkable. The nature of the Japanese government's response to the ultimatum was something close to contempt. Truman later said that they had sent back a "snotty answer" to the ultimatum. The English translation of the word "mokusatsu" was given as "reject." Its accurate translation was "to kill with silence," and that was their response.[5] In any event, the Japanese were not impressed with the Allies' ultimatum and had no intention of responding favorably to it.

After the bomb was dropped on Hiroshima, a second one on Nagasaki a few days later, and the Russians declared war on Japan, the Emperor Hirohito himself sent a surrender message.[6] On September 2, the battleship Missouri entered Tokyo Bay and General Douglas MacArthur presided over a surrender ceremony.

A major aspect of Truman's foreign policy came out of a 1946 telegram from George Kennan in Moscow to his Ambassador Harriman then in Washington. Harriman showed it to Secretary of State James Forrestal. Called the "Long Telegram," the message stated that Russia historically had pushed against its borders; it was an expansionist country. Kennan believed that it would be necessary for the West to push back at vulnerable places and prevent expansion until the Soviet Union collapsed from internal tensions which were aplenty in the post-war period. Or the Soviet Union might evolve in ways the United States might approve of. Kennan's view became the "containment policy" of several succeeding administrations. Finally, for many reasons, not simply the containment policy of the West, the stresses on the Soviet Union caused it to collapse in 1990-91.

Foreign Aid and Containment

President Truman's foreign policy was based on his conviction that the United States had to protect free nations that were threatened with repression. The Truman Doctrine, announced in 1947, provided aid to Greece and Turkey, two countries that were in danger of being swallowed up by the Soviets. In an address to a joint session of Congress on March 12, 1947, the President stated that the United States must aid and "support free peoples who are resisting attempted subjugation by armed minorities or by outside pressures."

The Marshall Plan, named for Secretary of State George C. Marshall, was another major foreign policy initiative. He presented the idea in a speech he delivered at Harvard in June, 1947. Marshall announced that this country intended to provide assistance to the devastated countries of Europe and called for these countries to plan and organize for the purpose. It will be remembered that Woodrow Wilson appointed Herbert Hoover to organize and carry out a food program for the war-devastated countries after the First World War. What was new and important about the Marshall Plan was that for the first time the United States assisted Europe as a single unit for purposes of receiving the aid. The Organization for Economic Cooperation and Development (the later OECD, originally OEEC) was the entity created. George Marshall received the Nobel Peace Prize for his work as architect of the Plan.

Just as Kennan predicted, the Soviets pressed at several points in Europe looking for places where it could expand. It harassed the Western powers in Berlin by closing the rail and autobahn access into the city in 1948. Truman instituted the Berlin airlift, an idea suggested by a British government official. The airlift brought food and other essential goods to the city for almost a year. Not only did this save Berlin but it responded forcefully to the Soviets. Eventually, the Soviets ended their blockade but watched for other opportunities to press against their borders.[7]

The Soviets threatened Norway by trying to entice it to join an alliance with it. Finland had already succumbed to Soviet pressure. Britain and the European powers were organizing a defensive alliance to which Norway could belong. In the United States, Harry Truman, a Democrat looking ahead to the 1948 election, had to deal with a Republican-dominated Congress some of whose members were openly critical of the President, charging that he was not effective in dealing with the Soviets. The President then told Congress that he thought this country should help the European alliance with military assistance and he asked Senator Arthur Vandenberg, a Republican and Chairman of the Senate Foreign Relations Committee, to take up the issue. The upshot was an agreement that the United States would form a military alliance with the European powers. The North American Treaty Organization was signed in 1949 and approved by the United States Senate.[8]

As American policy continued to practice "containment" in some of its foreign policy initiatives, knowledgeable people began to debate its merits. The scholar and historian Henry Kissinger discussed his view of "containment" explaining why he thought it was flawed as policy. First, Americans think that military power balances power, but that is not the case. Military power alone was insufficient for the purpose. Secondly, there needed to be alternative regional defenses. And thirdly, containment did not supply an adequate response to communist ideology.[9] There were factors other than military ones at work and being manipulated by the Soviets at this time. So, in the late 1940s and into the 1950s, President Truman confronted an increasingly threatening USSR. The Soviets had developed atomic weapons and detonated one in 1949. In 1957, they shot off Sputnik, the first earth satellite sent by any nation into space.

*President Harry S. Truman signing a proclamation
declaring a national emergency,
For the Korean "police action" December 16, 1950
Department of Defense, Author not known.*

President Truman had consistently supported the United Nations, and believed that when an agreement concerning post-war settlements was abrogated, as in the case of the 1950 invasion of South Korea by North Korea, the UN should enforce the agreement, militarily if necessary. Thus, the Korean "police action," as it was called, was proposed to the Security Council by the American delegation in 1950. As it happened, the Soviet representative to the UN had angrily walked out of a meeting of the Security Council, so that body voted in favor of the American resolution. American troops and those of some other nations were sent to South Korea and they drove the North Koreans back across the 38th Parallel. But this was deemed not a defensible position, and moreover, Chinese forces had joined the North. General Douglas MacArthur, appointed to direct the war in Korea, decided that the allied forces would have to drive the Chinese and North Korean forces north across the Yalu River in order to secure the relief of South Korea, and for a time this effort went forward. In the end, however, Chinese forces crossed the Yalu River heading south and these, combined with the North Korean army, would not be defeated quickly. The fighting ended when the newly elected President Eisenhower went to South Korea in 1952 to help set up the conditions for a truce. Peace came to the Koreas, but the Demilitarized Zone continues to divide North and South Korea. In 2008, the United States and others in the United Nations are deeply concerned about the development of nuclear weapons by the North.

Social Stresses

Truman's achievements at home were as significant as his foreign policy. He used the power of his presidency to promote civil rights for black people across a spectrum of political and social issues. At home in Independence, Missouri, he had become outraged by the work of the Ku Klux Klan in the State. At one time, the white-hooded gang had prevented Truman from being elected to be County Judge for Eastern Jackson County. Now at the urging of a group from the NAACP, the President created a civil rights committee by executive order, so that he would not have to go to Congress for authorization of such a body. The appointees were leaders in a variety of economic and social groups, both black and white. He assigned them the job of reporting to him what needed to be done by federal or state law to secure the rights of Americans to black people. They reported back to him after almost a year of study and analysis.

To further publicize his determination to make progress on civil rights for blacks, President Truman made an address to the NAACP standing at the Lincoln Memorial in Washington on June 29, 1947. Those in attendance thought he'd been courageous and thanked him.

Truman speaking at conference of NAACP, June 29, 1947
Photographer: Rowe, Abbie
Institutional Creator: National Park Service

The committee outlined four fundamental rights that should form the basis for the recommendations to come: a right to safety and security of the person, the right to citizenship and its privileges, the right to freedom of conscience and expression, and the right to equality of opportunity.[10] The committee recommended a federal anti-lynching law, a law to criminalize police brutality which was apt to be especially severe against blacks. There needed to be a law ending the poll tax. There should be a comprehensive voting rights law. There should be a law to end discrimination in the armed forces. This was an especially important issue to President Truman who had served in the armed forces himself and was outraged by the brutality brought upon returning black soldiers in some parts of the country in 1945. There needed to be a fair employment practices law and states should pass a fair education law. There should be a law prohibiting restrictive covenants. Some of these proposals were acted upon during Truman's presidency, such as the desegregation of the armed forces, the anti-lynching law, and criminalizing police brutality. The poll tax was outlawed by Constitutional Amendment. Other proposals became the agenda of the civil rights movement of the 1960s. Truman was the first President to grapple comprehensively with the necessity for laws to secure civil rights to American blacks.

The Economy

Truman struggled with issues in the domestic economy, dealing particularly with labor unions. The post-war period was one of labor-management disputes. The Democratic Congress passed the Taft-Hartley Act in 1947 which Truman vetoed but which veto Congress over-rode. Issues arose concerning under what circumstances a labor union could start a strike without penalty and force management to begin collective bargaining. The Taft-Hartley Act placed important restrictions on labor unions having to do with the right to strike. That Act required that a union observe a 60-day cooling-off period before undertaking a strike, and provided that the governing agency, the National Labor Relations Board, have the power to negotiate a peaceful settlement to a dispute. Although President Truman vetoed the Act and it was over-ridden, he had occasion to use it during the remainder of his administration. One occasion was during the Korean War when the steel industry unions threatened a strike. The President seized the steel mills to keep them working, but when this action was challenged before the Supreme Court, the Court said that he had exceeded the powers of the President.[11]

In 1948, the United Nations recognized the creation of the State of Israel. This was an important outcome from the nightmare of the Holocaust. The United States has viewed the creation and survival of Israel as a part of justice, but also as an important ally strategically located at the eastern end of the Mediterranean. The American government historically has supported Israel with economic and especially military assistance.

President Truman is held in high regard by students of American history and politics. Indeed, his accomplishments were remarkable as he completed the Roosevelt foreign policies and worked constructively to advance the civil rights efforts of Eleanor Roosevelt. The letters of Truman and Mrs. Roosevelt tell the story of their collaboration. The President appointed her to be the U.S. Representative to the UN Commission on Human Rights where her work as Chairman distinguished her as a world leader when the Commission drafted the UN Declaration of Human Rights.

INTERLUDE: FEAR OF COMMUNISM

The changing of the guard to the new administration in 1953 brought with it a decade of manifestations of the stresses on American society that flowed from the Second World War. The traumas from the war revealed suspicions, fear, and revealed some people in high places who couldn't cope emotionally with what appeared to be occurring. Senator Joseph McCarthy of Wisconsin was such a person. There were questions about the American war-time alliance with the Soviet Union which were exacerbated in the post-war years. Why had the Soviet Union become a major threat to us in such a brief period of time after 1945? In 1946, at President Truman's invitation, Winston Churchill had addressed the students of Westminster College in Fulton, Missouri and said that an "iron curtain" had been rung down across Europe dividing East and West and that the Soviets had set up governments on the East side that were brutal and totalitarian.

One other point about why the United States and the Soviet Union separated after the Second World War and could not come together thereafter until the USSR collapsed in 1990-91. That understanding came from the former Soviet Foreign Minister Maxim Litvinov who had been an important official in the Soviet government during the 1940s. He said to western scholars that the fundamental difference between the Soviets and the West was the conviction of Communists that there could be no reconciliation of communism with democracy; there was no way that communism and democracy could be compatible. He said that the cause was the "ideological conception prevailing here (USSR) of inevitability of conflict between Communist and capitalist worlds."[1] Communist theory had to be understood as irreconcilable with democracy because of the inevitability of a collapse of capitalism. The proletarian revolution would abolish a democratic system because capitalism was part and parcel of it.

Absolutist thinking has been seen before in the world in all sorts of political theories. Communism was such an absolutist theory. In the 1950s, the Soviet leadership was consumed with trying to fit Russian government policies into communist theory. The theory, Marxism-Leninism, must be correct; therefore action must be designed to fit into theory. Analysts of Soviet behavior in those years stressed the Communists' need for "correctness." Alternatively, Communist theorists tried to adjust the theory ever so slightly so that practice and theory could match.

In 1940, Congress passed the Smith Act which was intended to punish speech advocating the overthrow of the government by force and violence. The 1950s were years when people fearful of communism in the United States wondered whether there were traitors in the State Department, as alleged by Senator Joseph McCarthy, or whether it was a matter of false charges made by an irresponsible Senator. The Senator made impassioned speeches to his fellow Senators; held up pages purported to be lists of names of people in government he suspected of communist leanings. President Eisenhower deplored the allegations, but the Senate, independent as it was, continued. In several years, the uproar played itself out and some faithful government employees struggled to recover from the impugning of their integrity, their good names having been dragged through the mud. The reputations of several, like that of John Stewart Service, a valued foreign service officer in China, were destroyed. Service was fired by the State Department but was reinstated by the Supreme Court. The offense Service committed was to correctly predict that the Chinese Communists would defeat and route the Chinese Nationalist forces from China. In the hysteria over communism in government, he was charged with "losing" China. The Senate officially censured McCarthy several years later, but the damage was done.

The issue of communism in our government did not go away easily because there were people who had in fact betrayed the United States: Julius and Ethel Rosenberg, for example. Then there were people who were drawn into communist theory by academic or theoretical discussion. Alger Hiss, an employee of the State Department was such a person. Whittaker Chambers, not a government employee, was an acquaintance of Hiss and was drawn into a communist cell. He blew the whistle on Hiss, and the latter was tried and convicted of perjury for lying about his connections to the Communist movement. He was sent to prison for a few years, then released. Chambers' book *Witness* explained his own thinking about how he got involved with communists. His book described how some 35mm film rolls which could incriminate Hiss were hidden in a hollowed-out pumpkin kept outside behind his Maryland home in the fall of 1948.

How to distinguish people who advocated communism in theory, as one might in an academic discussion, from people who might be traitors, might be dangerous to the country? The Supreme Court heard several cases brought to it under the Smith Act. In *Dennis v United* States[2] the Court upheld the Smith Act as constitutional, and thereby allowed a number of convictions for conspiracy to stand. But in a later case, *Yates v United* States[3] the Justices concluded that there was a difference between active advocacy urging the overthrow of the government by force and violence, and merely academic or theoretical advocacy which is protected by the First Amendment. Some communists convicted of treason appealed lower court decisions to the Supreme Court and these were the distinctions the

Court made in determining that some of those charged were engaged in active advocacy, others were not and should be exonerated.

The confounding events, however, would not go away. Richard Nixon, when a member of the House, served on the House Un-American Activities Committee, notorious under the leadership of Martin Dies for its accusations of Hollywood actors as being left-wing, maybe communist in orientation. Nixon became Chairman of the Committee in the late 1940s, and made a reputation for himself. He believed that some of the people the Committee investigated were a threat to the nation. In 1950, Nixon won a Senate seat, and later still was chosen by Eisenhower to join him on the Republican ticket as a Vice Presidential candidate. They won the election of 1952 and won re-election in 1956.

Scholars began to study the phenomenon of communist cells trying to learn how extensive this movement was in the country. The theory of communism had been around for some time, but the public did not have a clear understanding of how communists differed from socialists, as in Britain, for example. Moreover, there were the Anarchists who wanted no government at all. It was believed that President McKinley had been assassinated by an Anarchist in 1901. One theory was that while there were communist cells in various parts of the country, they really did not succeed in gaining strength because members came to dislike communist methods. Americans had long engaged in voluntary groups that had open memberships. The communist style of group work was disciplined, closed, and secretive, contrary to the practices of traditional voluntary associations in this country. Mid-century scholarship reminded the country that Alexis De Tocqueville was right in his book *Democracy in America* where he said that the way Americans get things done is through their voluntary associations. Fear of communism has subsided since the Soviet Union itself abandoned it in 1990.

DWIGHT DAVID EISENHOWER
1953-1961

Dwight Eisenhower was a great hero of the Second World War, had led the invasion of Normandy on D-Day and in almost a year, the war was over in Europe. In 1952, the Korean War was moving into an uncertain stage, with President Truman opposing an invasion of China to take on the Communist regime there, and General MacArthur unable to conclude the "police action" to restore the security of South Korea. Americans looked to Eisenhower to bring the Korean War to an end. This was the immediate project on his agenda as he came into office. The solution was a truce and the creation of a demilitarized zone between South and North Korea at the 38th Parallel, a boundary line originally set by international agreement after the Second World War.

Foreign Policy

After the war years, with the Roosevelt initiatives to create institutions for collective security and the Truman years dealing with the aggressiveness of the Soviet Union while committing the United States to helping Europe recover, the foreign policy agenda for the 1950s burgeoned with obligations. In addition to the treaties in which the United States was already a member, new treaties and agreements were concluded with nations around the world. Some were designed to promote economic benefits, such as trade and aid, while others were purely military agreements designed to protect the member nations. The Southeast Asia Treaty Organization (SEATO) was an example of the latter.

Dwight Eisenhower was born in a rural environment in northern Texas and raised in Abilene, Kansas, as his father moved around trying to make a living. Dwight was one of six brothers in the family. He loved sports while at school, but could not afford college where he might have been able to pursue his love of sports. So, like many poor young men he applied for an appointment to both the Naval Academy and West Point. He won the opening at West Point and graduated from the Military Academy with "middling grades," according to a biographer.[1] He served at a number of posts, including the Philippines, Panama and Hawaii. His superior officer in Panama, Fox Conner, taught him the importance of learning the "art of commanding multinational coalitions."[2] Conner was sure that Germany again would be ready to fight European countries, and that the United States would be allied with them.

While Eisenhower was trained in the arts of war, he was very glad after 1945 to turn to the works of peace. He returned to a hero's welcome after the war. He was asked to be President of Columbia University, which he accepted, and a few years later he was touted to be an ideal candidate for President of the United States. As a military leader, he had stayed out of politics, at least in terms of partisanship. So to think about running for President, he had to consider to which political party he belonged. In due course, he announced that he would run for President as a Republican.

Preserving the Peace

Eisenhower inherited from the Truman and Roosevelt administrations commitments to international organizations intended to resist the Soviet Union without going to war with it if possible. The commitments were intended to promote peace and maintain alliances with friendly nations. These formed a major part of his agenda as he came into office, and over a period of 8 years he enlarged the reach of American involvement in the world. The advice of his superior officer in Panama was useful not only in time of war, but also in time of peace when preserving the peace was essential. He chose John Foster Dulles as his Secretary of State, a man of whom Winston Churchill said he is, "the only bull who carried his own China closet with him."[3]

Dulles was a very large man, heavy in appearance and demeanor, even sometimes rude. Nevertheless, he was effective in international relations because he understood it. Foreign affairs ran in the family. His grandfather, John W. Foster, Secretary of State in the 19th Century and his uncle Robert Lansing, Woodrow Wilson's Secretary of State, were both influential in his development. The young Dulles was the drafter of the infamous reparations agreement made at the Paris Peace Conference that brought the First World War to an end.[4] Significantly, Dulles became a partner of the New York law firm Sullivan and Cromwell whose business was primarily engaged in international finance. Dulles believed that religious principles should guide the policies of his country. He had a close working relationship with the President, sharing Ike's approach to American foreign policy. The President's role as chief diplomat was not in doubt, however.

President Eisenhower's long experience in the Army formed the basis for his organization of the White House office. With the Cold War in full cry, and with the opponents and their intentions clearly understood, the President used all his skills of organization and administration to set up a system that would protect the United States while aggressively promoting his objectives in foreign policy. In addition to his foreign policy team Eisenhower created a special assistant for national security affairs to head up the National Security

Council. That Council was given separate boards for operations and planning, and met once a week.[5]

Eisenhower put forward a New Look in foreign and defense policy that included a modification of the "containment policy." It emphasized regional alliances to avoid the polarity that was thought to dominate international politics in the mid-century. The President was concerned about the implications of that policy, however, with its commitment of military forces and enormous expenditures for the indefinite future. He did not want to engage American troops in more wars like that in Korea, which was officially ended in July 1953. Yet he had members of Congress urging a tougher approach to the Soviets and more awareness of the communist government in China. The public was fearful. Senator John Kennedy, who was to run for President in 1960, urged a tougher stance against the new leadership in the USSR after Stalin's death in 1953. Lavrenty Beria and Georgi Malenkov succeeded the dictator. Malenkov spoke at the funeral of Stalin and stated that a new era of "peaceful coexistence" could occur. Churchill urged Eisenhower to meet with them, but the President did not see any substantive issues which he could discuss with the Soviets.

Eisenhower called for careful and detailed study by his staff and concluded that he would support the Democrats' "collective security" policy. The New Look called for superior military forces but contained budget cuts that would be realized through the reduction of conventional forces, and the maintenance of nuclear weapons. Dulles advanced his threat of "massive retaliation;"[6] nuclear weapons could be used if the Soviets threatened the United States and its interests with aggression.

The President and his Secretary of State were concerned about Southeast Asia, particularly the role of China in the region. China had been taken over by the communist regime of MaoTse Tung whose military forces had driven the Chinese Nationalist regime out of China and to Formosa, now called Taiwan. At the same time, as an historical process of decolonization in Asia, Africa and the Middle East developed in the middle of the century, the former French colony of Indo-China, now called Vietnam, saw hostilities between the political party of Ho Chi Minh, the Vietminh in the North and Ngo Dinh Diem's regime in the South for control of the whole of Vietnam. Eisenhower and Dulles determined to create a defense alliance for the region, so Dulles negotiated with seven other nations to form SEATO, the Southeast Asia Treaty Organization.

The Taiwan Straits became another focal point for American policy, and gave credence to the view that because the Americans and the Chinese did not communicate except by military threat, the Chinese were bold enough to begin a military attack against Quemoy and Matsu,[7] two islands off the coast of China. The islands had no strategic or other value to the United States, but had political value to the Chinese for threat purposes. Eisenhower acted to deter China and respond to Congress which was much concerned that the U.S. was not tough enough toward China. The government signed a Mutual Defense Treaty with Formosa (Taiwan) and persuaded Congress to adopt the Formosa Resolution which gave the President authority to respond to Chinese aggression should it threaten. The Administration, expressing its own brinkmanship language, also began to consider using a nuclear weapon. For whatever reason,

Dwight D. Eisenhower

Chou en-lai, speaking at a conference at Bandung, made concilia-tory statements so the U.S. indicated its interest in a meeting. One was set up in Warsaw where ambassadors would meet and talk. After this exchange of threats and nerves, there was no nuclear war.

The arrangements of the European governments to counter the ever-present Soviet threat finally concluded with a defense arrangement that would include West Germany which was made part of NATO. A political agreement accompanied the military accord. At a conference in 1954, the nine powers, including the United States, agreed to a Western European Union including Italy and West Germany. The West Germans agreed not to produce weapons, bombers, and warships and in response the other participants recognized West Germany as a sovereign nation. Thus, the Allied occupation of West Germany was ended ten years after it had begun.[8]

The Middle East was the remaining area where the United States was eager to resolve hostilities. Here the Administration was less successful than in Europe or in Asia. All sorts of forces were at work: Arabs and Israelis, some Arab countries versus others, and Arab nationalism struggling with European colonial powers. Arab nationalism was the dream of Colonel Gamal Abdel Nasser. He was able to overthrow King Farouk of Egypt in 1952, thus getting rid of a monarchy, and he asserted that Arab countries should join together to form a pan-Arab alliance. This became the United Arab Republic consisting only of Egypt and Syria. Congress granted to the President $200 million in aid and authority to act in case of military action by any aggressors in the Middle East. This grant of authority was called the Eisenhower Doctrine, and it followed up on the Truman Doctrine of aid to Greece and Turkey in the 1940s.

The Middle East was more involved in its own hostilities than in concerns about what the Soviets might do. The indigenous conflicts led to hostile reactions against U.S. policies. Moreover, Nasser was a smart leader who knew how to manage his country and his neighbors. Eisenhower and Dulles offered Nasser money for the construction of the Aswan Dam to be built on the Nile. It would provide electric power and protection from the annual flooding of the Nile while promoting agriculture. Various parties vehemently opposed the promise by the U.S. to help: Congressmen from the South who visualized competition from Egyptian cotton, and Israel which considered this to be help to a sworn enemy. Nasser announced the recognition of his country to China, and tried to get aid from the Soviets, and these actions were enough to convince Dulles to cancel the deal. Now everybody was mad.

Nasser, not to be put down, declared in July, 1956 that Egypt had nationalized the Suez Canal, taking ownership away from a British company that had managed the waterway for many years. Nasser said that he had to do this to collect tolls which would pay for the work on the Aswan Dam. This, of course, also threatened the oil supplies for Europe. Dulles urged Anthony Eden, British Foreign Minister, to agree to an international consortium to run the canal and pay compensation to Egypt. Eden would have none of it. Britain and France decided on a secret attack, to be carried out by Israel, to seize the Sinai and Gaza. The Europeans demanded that Nasser withdraw and when he refused, the British and French began air and naval attacks against Egypt. Nasser's response was to sink more than fifty ships in the canal which assured that it would not be a useful waterway to anyone for some years.

These events marked the most serious situation to occur between the United States and its European allies. The British and Dulles had a misunderstanding. Anthony Eden thought that Dulles had indicated American approval of the plan to deal with Egypt but this was not true in the minds of the Americans. Eisenhower and Dulles were furious. They knew nothing of the military plan and could not imagine why the Europeans would take such an action just before the Presidential election of 1956. As the historian George Herring explained,

The Suez affair was one of the most complex and dangerous of Cold War crises. Walking a tightrope over numerous conflicting forces, Eisenhower did manage to avert war with the Soviet Union and limit the damage to relations with the Arab states. On the other hand, America's relations with its major allies plunged to their lowest point in years. Washington and London each believed that they had been double-crossed.[9]

Eisenhower's response to the situation was to look for ways to strengthen pro-Western governments that were stable in the region, providing them with economic and military assistance, in keeping with the Eisenhower Doctrine. He indicated that if the Soviets intervened in Middle East affairs and if Nasser were to work with them, the United States was prepared to take military action.

Social Stresses

As can be seen, Eisenhower's managerial style was to let subordinates take responsibility for their departments and the policies thereof. He left the execution of foreign affairs to John Foster Dulles, the Secretary of State, and took a similar position toward his other department heads. He was also one to let lower levels of government fulfill their responsibilities before the federal government became involved. There were occasions when this style of leadership was thought to be inadequate; the President appeared to be too laid back. A case in point had to do with the issue of school desegregation in Little Rock, Arkansas' Central School. In the years after the landmark case of Brown v. Board of Education of Topeka in which the Supreme Court declared that racially segregated schools were "inherently unequal" and unconstitutional under the Fourteenth Amendment's provision of the "equal protection of the laws," there was an effort in Little Rock to follow the law.

The Little Rock School Board had designed a plan for gradual integration of the schools to begin in 1957. But when school opened in September, the Governor of Arkansas, Orval Faubus, took a state's rights position and ordered the Arkansas National Guard to surround the school to keep the black children out. The Mayor of Little Rock appealed to the President to send troops and Eisenhower ordered 1,000 members of the101st Airborne Division to go to Little Rock and enforce the desegregation rule. He also federalized the Arkansas National Guard, thus putting it under federal control. It was an important test case as to whether states that still had segregated schools would integrate them. And it was a test case whether state officials would recognize the supremacy of the federal law over state laws. There were some who thought Eisenhower had acted too slowly, that with swift action in sending the troops he could have stopped the flouting of the federal law in its earliest days. The President, for his part, believed in States rights and thought the matter should be allowed to work itself out.

After a year of the presence of the federal troops; Central School was integrated and the Little Rock Nine black students completed a year of their education at Central School. In the following years, however, there was continuing litigation and Central was closed at one time. A "private" school was created for white students. Some went there while others left and went to school elsewhere. Some families moved away. Nevertheless, the sad history of racial hostility toward integrated education for black and white children could no longer find a place in the law.

President Eisenhower was in Colorado when he had a heart attack and was taken to the hospital there. Richard Nixon carried on for him; the President recovered and went back to Washington to run for re-election. This event brought about the Presidential Disability Amendment to the Constitution that established the procedures through which an orderly transfer of power must occur until a President can resume the responsibilities of the office. The

President recovered and after he was re-elected to a second term he went on to another four years of service to his country.

The Economy

The President's approach to economic policy was to provide leadership that would restore a peacetime economy and prevent major fluctuations in the business cycle. Several conditions supported this position. Under the Bretton Woods agreement made at the end of the war, other currencies were pegged to the dollar, which was based on a gold standard of $35 per ounce. The purpose was for the U.S. to lead the international economic order, and indeed during the 1950s and 1960s, the U.S. dominated the world economy. Also, the period was one of low unemployment and low inflation, and the Gross Domestic Product was strong. So Eisenhower and his successors, Kennedy, Johnson and for a time Nixon were considered good stewards of the economy. As Dolan, Frendreis, and Tatalovich point out, "When Eisenhower assumed the presidency, the United States was by far the world's premier economic powerhouse."[10] This country produced almost half of the manufactured goods in the world. The President, a true conservative, appointed Arthur Burns and other businessmen to his Council of Economic Advisers. The era was called one of "economic orthodoxy."

The National Defense Highway system was planned and approved by the Eisenhower administration, and was adopted by Congress in 1957. The Interstate network was a response to popular demand. It contributed, as did the G.I. Bill adopted by the Truman Administration, to urban sprawl but certainly it was in keeping with the inseparability of the American and his car. By the end of the Century, maintaining the Interstate system was very costly. The alternative to heavy use of the Interstates is mass transit, and in some cities the train is the preferred mode of transportation because transit has been modernized for speed and comfort. However, continued maintenance of the tax-supported Interstates will continue to be expensive. Some of these highways are made toll roads, which reduces some of the maintenance cost; the vast majority of the Interstates run through states to connect cities. New funding mechanisms may be in the future of these highways.

When he left office in 1961, President Eisenhower addressed the American people and warned them of the dangers of a powerful "military-industrial complex" which he considered a threat to the country because it could get beyond the control of any branch of government. It consisted of the defense industry, the Defense Department, congressional committees, and covert agencies like the CIA. Eisenhower, an internationalist, did not consider American commitments around the world as supporting the military-industrial complex even though many of those commitments involved providing American weapons to other countries. He simply believed that there must be no misuse of power in this government of checks and balances, and that is the message he meant to convey.

THE ECONOMY IN MID-CENTURY

The United States was prosperous in the 1950s and 1960s. The post-war boom brought with it growing production of the materials people needed to buy and furnish, even embellish their homes. During the War, there was a pent-up demand for all kinds of goods, led by housing. The G.I. Bill gave low-interest loans to war veterans and this contributed substantially to the boom. Not that there weren't economic problems; immediately after the war a short recession developed because of the changes, radical in some cases, from government investment in hardware for war to a civilian peacetime economy. Because of higher tax rates for the highest-income people and the relative strength of unions with their bargaining power, the people producing material goods for the American public had income protection. Prosperity meant that people who had never before been able to own a home now were living the American dream, thanks to the G.I. Bill. Security for older people was provided by Social Security, and for those who lost their jobs, there was unemployment compensation. All of these benefits were creatures of the New Deal and its laws passed in the 1930s.

Paul Krugman, in his book *The Conscience of a Liberal,* explains,

> *In sum, then, the political economy of the United States in the 1950s and into the 1960s was far more favorable to income-equalizing economic policies than it had been during*

the Long Gilded Age [1870s to 1930s according to Krugman].
The welfare state was no longer considered radical; instead, those
who wanted to dismantle it were regarded as cranks. There was
no longer a large class of disenfranchised immigrant workers.
The South was, conditionally and temporarily, on the side of
economic equality, as long as that didn't translate into racial
equality. And a powerful union movement had the effect of
mobilizing lower-income voters.[1]

Dwight Eisenhower wrote in a letter to his brother Edgar in 1954, "Should any political party attempt to abolish social security, unemployment insurance, and eliminate labor laws and farm programs, you would not hear of that party again in our political history."[2] He thought that anyone who wanted to change these laws was "stupid." Thus government policies that in the '30s were considered liberal, even radical, came to be respectable in the 1950s.

In the years following the Great Depression, Presidents sought to respond to economic struggles by using what powers they had to exert control over the economic system. Franklin Roosevelt appointed economic advisers to counsel him on economic conditions; this approach was made into law early in the Truman Administration when Congress passed the Employment Act of 1946. The law gave the President the responsibility for managing the national economy, and formally created the Council of Economic Advisers in the Executive Office of the President to assist him. The Council's members are appointed by the President. From this time forward, there was no doubt about the President's role in using fiscal policy (taxing and spending) to encourage employment levels or to rein in inflation. Meanwhile, monetary policy, the other wheel in managing the economy, was the role of the Federal Reserve System to increase or decrease the money supply. The Federal Reserve Board of Governors is appointed by the President.

From the perspective of 2008, some of the ideas of economists in mid-Century make us thoughtful. The Keynsian view of deficit spending and lower taxes was ultimately rejected by Franklin Roosevelt primarily because he could not imagine any policy that would depart from balancing the budget. He could not cause a balanced budget to happen during the Depression, but he was sure that that was the goal the government should pursue as soon as the economy was restored to normal again.[3] He considered his use of pump-priming as a purely temporary measure to provide jobs and improve the infrastructure of the country.

Along came Milton Friedman in 1962 with his book *Capitalism and Freedom.*[4] His approach to economics was to say that the road to freedom was capitalism, and the less regulated business enterprise was, the better. Ultimately, he argued that unfettered business and industry provided freedom for everyone. He was the first to say that government is the problem, which became a mantra in the 1980s and 1990s. Friedman's theory was given a full trial with Reagan's Presidency and for twenty years thereafter until the deregulation and Keynesian tax reduction policies in the George W. Bush years had run their course. This approach to the American economy also included the practice of deficit spending by government, Ronald Reagan's policy. It was reversed by President Clinton when he balanced the national budget at the end of his second term. Many people applauded that accomplishment. But with the wars following the attacks on 9-11, deficit spending to pay for them was restored. Meanwhile, President Bush pursued a policy of tax reduction.

Historically, national economic policies of Presidents do not provide sure guidelines to reduce inflation or raise the level of employment in the country. Much as economic theorists try to understand the business cycle and the economic behavior of the American public at any given time, their conclusions usually prove of limited value over time. Everyone agrees that there is a business cycle and that it behaves in a certain way at any given period, and certain kinds of treatment may bring about a hoped-for response of the system. But as many Presidents have discovered, no economic theory works all of the time and therefore it is best to approach treatment of the system pragmatically.

Presidents Eisenhower and Kennedy
Eisenhower Library Photo No. 62-2-1USN
PD-USGOV

JOHN FITZGERALD KENNEDY

1961-1963

John Kennedy was another war hero. He had served in the Navy during the Second World War and was famous for his exploits personified in the story of PT Boat 109 when he saved his crew. He also wrote a book *Profiles in Courage* which was published after he came home from the war. He was a member of a prominent family, the Kennedys of Boston and Hyannisport. His father had hoped that his first son, Joseph, would run for President of the United States and was shattered when Joseph was killed in the war. John and his brothers Robert and Edward all had ambitions in that direction and John, the oldest of the three, decided to run for President in 1960. Kennedy ran with Lyndon Johnson from Texas as his vice-presidential running mate and they defeated Vice President Richard Nixon.

Foreign Policy

Kennedy's inherited agenda was the international leadership role of the United States but he added his own views to the picture in which he saw himself as President. In his election campaign, he stressed his belief that the country had lost its military position of dominance and that this must be corrected. In his inaugural address, he boasted that his generation, born in this century, brought new concepts of freedom, a new agenda and a new view of America. He warned the Soviet Union that " we will bear any burden, ..." to ensure liberty in this country and in the world. Whether in response to that or not, the Soviets decided to build a wall to divide East and West Berlin; the wall stood from 1961 until 1989 when Germans on both sides of it tore it down. This was possible because the Soviet puppet premier of East Germany had fled to the Soviet Union in the waning days of that regime. A year later, Berlin was free and the Soviet Union as a political entity collapsed.

The 1960s was a decade of expectation by the leaders of government. A decade of hubris. David Halberstam describes the Kennedy appointees in *The Best and the Brightest* as well-educated, elegant men who saw in Kennedy a leader of intelligence and strength who could take the country to the moon, both literally and figuratively. They were men who could believe in the idea of limited war but could prepare the country for the ultimate war if need be. They could believe in their own superiority over the Soviet leadership. Joseph Stalin had died in the early '50s and Party Chairman Khrushchev had disgraced himself in the UN's Security Council by banging his shoe on his desk to express his "nyet." The posture of the Democrats was an emphatic anti-communism and a new nationalism. Hence Kennedy's position on needing more weapons; especially, he sought missile development. Part of this picture was his decision that the United States should go to the moon, develop the rockets necessary to carry a man to the moon and bring him back safely to earth.

Kennedy took responsibility for approving a military attack by Cuban exiles at the Bay of Pigs. While the original thinking for this plan came out of the last year of the Eisenhower administration and was developed by the CIA, some people commented that Eisenhower would not have approved it as it was carried out. A short while after the fiasco, Kennedy called Eisenhower and asked him to meet him at Camp David. They talked about what had happened, and Ike asked the President whether he had run the plan by the National Security Council. "Kennedy confessed that he had not had a full meeting of the NSC to discuss and criticize the plans. He seemed to Eisenhower to be 'very frank but also very subdued and more than a little bewildered.'"[1]

However, a year later, the President had an opportunity to show his mettle as a military man, a diplomat and a master of bluff. This occurred when Soviet missiles, a major threat, were seen by satellite on the ground in Cuba, ninety miles from the United States. Moreover, the Navy reported to the President that other Soviet ships were on their way to Cuba believed to be bringing more missiles. With the help of his brother Bobby and the ExComm of Cabinet members and men from the military leaders in government, Jack Kennedy devised a plan to order a blockade of American ships (he called it a quarantine, a blockade is an act of war) to intercept the incoming vessels, board them, and order them to turn around and go back whence they came. Implicit in the order was that if they did not observe the order, American ships would fire on them and American air power was available. He then announced to Congress, the Soviets and the American people what he had done.[2] Whether this threat to attack the Soviet ships would cause them to turn around was a question on the mind of every alert American during the several days the drama unfolded.

The Strategic Air Command during this crisis had ordered its bombers from numerous bases around the country into the air where they stayed over the several days of the crisis. One or two ships were boarded by American naval personnel. Khrushchev sent a letter of response to Kennedy which seemed to reject the order, but sent another letter the next day expressing compliance with Kennedy's order. Kennedy and Khrushchev agreed that the USSR would remove the missiles from Cuba, the United States promised not to invade Cuba and the two would secure an agreement together with the Secretary General of the United Nations. What was not made public is that their agreement included a promise that Kennedy would order the removal of U.S. offensive missiles from Turkey, a proviso that observers have thought was the original intention of Khrushchev in putting Soviet missiles in Cuba.[3] The Cuban Missile Crisis was the closest Americans ever got to a hot war with the Soviet Union.

Since the late 1940s, member nations in the United Nations had been searching for ways to limit the spread of nuclear weapons and to limit the possible use of them by any nuclear power. Kennedy too had been working for some time on the idea of nuclear non-proliferation. He hoped to show the world that the United States sought peace with all nations but knew that the best protection would be restraint on the part of all nations. To begin such an effort, he consulted with his advisers, particularly Robert McNamara, Secretary of Defense who had the intelligence and skills to offer a solid plan to the President. Nuclear non-proliferation would require a willingness by the participating nations to agree to a negative. It would be necessary for signatories to such a concept to refrain from selling or giving other nations the technology to develop nuclear weapons. And to get to that point it would be necessary for nuclear nations to agree to ban the testing of nuclear weapons. The test ban treaty finally agreed to was the product of the managerial brain of Robert McNamara and the political necessity perceived by Kennedy.[4] It was devised in the months before Kennedy was killed.

The assassination of John Kennedy was a shock to the nation, but his agenda continued to guide the government of Lyndon Johnson and its successors. The necessity for the nuclear powers to pursue the non-proliferation of nuclear weapons continued to be at the top of the national agenda for decades. As more nations developed the science of nuclear power and the urgency to prevent the spread of weapons that would use it, the project became more and more difficult. Moreover, it became vital to persuade nations developing their own nuclear capability to desist. Preventing further proliferation continued to be essential to American foreign policy and military preparedness well into the Twenty-first Century.

Lyndon Johnson taking the oath after Kennedy was killed.
Author: Cecil W. Stoughton, White House Press Office, Date: 1963-11-22

To The Moon

Kennedy's initiative of space flight and the exploration of the moon was greeted enthusiastically by scientists and the public alike. It was an enormous challenge; the resources available were knowledge about rockets and the belief of many people that America could reach the goal. While Kennedy and many military leaders believed that the country needed an outpost in space for national security purposes, the prospect of exploring where man had never been before fed a spirit of adventure in the nation. Eventually, the outpost idea led to the building of an International Space Station, but the immediate project was to develop a space-faring vehicle. The earliest space exploration had been done in a capsule flown around the earth by an astronaut. The rocket power to lift that vehicle out of the earth's gravity had been proven, and the capsule could return to earth landing in the ocean where it and the astronaut could be recovered. The moon project, however, called for sustained flight and the ability of astronauts to maneuver in space, and survive for days in a space craft. Moreover, the scientists and engineers would have to figure out a way for a craft to land on the moon, then leave it somehow and return to earth. In addition to all that, what would the moon be like?

Moon Landing
Image courtesy NASA
(NASA photo Ids AS11-40-5863 and AS11-40-5868)

The Apollo program built the first crafts designed to journey to the moon. Americans became excited about the trip to the moon when it was announced in 1969 that the first Apollo mission to land on the moon would occur during the summer. Through the previous year or two, several initial flights to test vehicles and the astronauts showed how difficult this program would be if it were to reach its goal. There was the fire that broke out as one of the Apollo craft sat on the launch pad. It was not scheduled to go that day; the plan was only to test the craft. The fire occurred so fast it killed three astronauts before anyone could act to put it out.

In July, 1969, however, Apollo 11 with three astronauts on board was launched for the trip to the moon. It was an amazing feat of engineering and physics. Apollo 11 reached moon orbit and it spun off the landing craft, called the Eagle, which was to land two astronauts on the moon. It did so, as one of the men reported, "Houston, the Eagle has landed." In another communication, he reported "Tranquility Base here." Then Neil Armstrong went out to test the moon's soil and see how the walking would be. He said, "One small step for man; one giant leap for mankind." The world was watching and it was cheering. Americans were thrilled with this magnificent achievement. The memory of President Kennedy burned brightly that day.

LYNDON BAINES JOHNSON
1963-1969

The accession of Lyndon Johnson to the Presidency was uncomfortable to many, not least to Johnson himself who was unsure of himself and how he would relate to the Kennedy team he would inherit. Here was somebody with roots in the West, with a booming voice, a Texas accent and a folksy manner of speech. However, he knew his way around Washington, particularly about how to get things done. Johnson had been Majority Leader of the Senate, a position which enabled him to advance the programs of the Democrats.

The new President had been a great admirer of Franklin Roosevelt who had given him his first job with the government. The job was to organize the New Deal's National Youth Administration in Texas whose purpose was to help young people finish school or college with a part-time job on campus. It helped young people who were not in school too, with small public works projects that would provide them some income while improving their communities. It was a challenge to the young Lyndon because he'd had no administrative experience. But the job appealed to him because it would help blacks and Mexican-Americans. He'd been a teacher after he finished college; his students often were poor kids of mixed races. They needed all the help they could get. This appointment met another need of the young man, his need to fulfill his deeply-felt sympathy for poor people generally. His superiors in Washington thought him energetic and imaginative, said he would "go places."[1]

Lyndon Johnson was personally "overwhelming." As described by Henry Kissinger, he was huge, hulking. Physically large, he was forceful in his manner. He had the baffling practice of reaching out with great sympathy and compassion to help people who needed it, but suddenly withdrawing support if his earnest desire conflicted with his other deep passion, to advance his power and position. This was a difficult problem for Johnson because in politics he was always confronting the possibility that his support of a bill, for example, would displease important people among his constituents. He never really conquered his difficulty with duplicity, and this made him distrusted by people who had dealings with him that were less than satisfactory.[2]

The Civil Rights Act of 1964

Describing such a person does not prepare one for the phenomenal accomplishments of his five years as President. Having spent years in the House and Senate opposed to all civil rights legislation, he now had to embrace anti-lynching bills, bills to require places of public accommodation to be open to all races, and bills to secure public education to all children regardless of race. Johnson supported passage of the 1964 Civil Rights Act.

The bill had been proposed by President Kennedy and his administration, but after his death, in an atmosphere of widespread public sympathy for the Kennedy programs, the civil rights bill already introduced in Congress was actually strengthened. Robert Kennedy, still Attorney General in the early Johnson years, worked with the Senate Minority Leader Everett Dirksen to draft a bill that they both thought could pass. A major aspect of the strengthening of the bill was the recognition by Senators that the Supreme Court's decisions regarding civil rights issues had up until that time dealt with "state action," that is, action by a state in violation of the 14th Amendment's equal protection of the laws clause. Senators, and the Attorney General, Robert F. Kennedy, realized that they needed a stronger vehicle to carry civil rights legislation beyond interpretations based on the 14th Amendment. That is when they hit upon the commerce clause as the best vehicle for civil rights.[3] It had always been broadly interpreted by the Supreme Court, but the same could not be said of the 14th Amendment.

The bill provided that businesses in interstate commerce could not deny services to anyone regardless of race, color or creed. It proscribed discrimination in places of public accommodation like hotels motels, restaurants, entertainment facilities, and the like. Moreover, it had a provision prohibiting discrimination where the employer is engaged in interstate commerce, and it specified that there could be no discrimination in admission to schools and colleges. The bill prohibited discrimination in federally-funded programs.[4]

The civil rights bill survived an attempt in the House to keep it from being sent to the floor so that the whole House could consider it. The members who favored it made a motion to discharge it from the Committee considering it, and that brought the desired result. The bill advanced to the House floor where it was debated and passed. In the Senate, however, a different tactic was used by the Southern Senators, led by Richard Russell of Georgia. This was a filibuster, a process of Senators talking it to death. This time-honored procedure provides that any Senator can be recognized to speak and do so indefinitely, handing off to other like-minded Senators, talking about anything, even though there is a rule about germaneness. The only way to stop a filibuster is to get a motion for cloture, that is, for the Senate to agree that debate must be stopped so that a bill can be considered and voted on. A certain number of Senators must agree on the motion for cloture (67 in 1964), and then each Senator can talk for one more hour. Ultimately, however, the presiding officer of the Senate must determine that an end to discussion has occurred, and that a vote must be taken on the bill itself.

This whole process was used for the Civil Rights Bill of 1964. The debate lasted 5 months, the filibuster lasted for more than 2 months and then, with the agreement of the Minority Leader of the Senate, Everett Dirksen, (R. Illinois), a vote to close debate was taken.[5] There was much public interest in this vote; radio and television followed the voting. The Civil Rights Bill passed by a narrow margin, but it was a victory for those who favored civil rights. The President signed the Bill into law on July 4, 1964.

The Economy

President Johnson got a strong vote of confidence in the November presidential election, and from this point on, he used the power of his office to advance much legislation which had been discussed in Congress for years and had been on his personal agenda for years. He talked about a Great Society and brought forward the Elementary and Secondary Education Act which was passed in 1965, and in the next year the Voting Rights Act which prohibited discrimination in registering to vote, as well as in actually casting a ballot. In cases where the right to vote was obstructed, the U.S. Attorney General's office could step in and compel observance of the law. In 1968, a Fair Housing Act was passed by Congress, supporting non-discrimination in purchasing, selling or renting of housing.

Johnson speech introducing the "Great Society" plan at the University of Michigan.
http://photolab.lbjlib.utexas.edu/detail.asp?741
Serial Number: C387-8-WH64

In addition to federal funding for local school districts, the Education Act of 1965 provided scholarships, grants and work-study programs for college students. It provided bilingual education for Hispanic children while they learned English. There was federal support for Special Education for children with learning disabilities. Head Start originated during the 1960s. There were some very significant health programs adopted during these years. Health care for elderly people had been discussed for years, notably in the Truman years, but the Medicare program was not adopted until 1965. Medicaid was also adopted to provide health care for the indigent. During these years too, there was significant funding for medical research.

Other important new federal programs adopted in the Great Society years included food stamps for low-income people, and a school breakfast program for poor children. The Model Cities program was begun, intended to help cities improve their poor neighborhoods where infrastructure was needed. For the environment, the Clear Air Act, the Water Quality and Clean Water Restoration Acts, the 1965 Solid Waste Disposal Act and the Motor Vehicle Air Pollution Control Act were adopted. There was a significant increase in Social Security funding inspired by President Johnson, the result of which was to lift some 12 million elderly citizens above the poverty level.

There was much political opposition to the "War on Poverty," especially as manifested in the Office of Economic Opportunity, but it is notable that Presidents after Johnson have recommended that Congress fund its programs. As for the major reliance Americans placed on transportation, the Johnson years saw the adoption of the Urban Mass Transit Act that helped modernize bus and train systems in cities throughout the country.[6]

Foreign Policy

The tragedy of Lyndon Johnson's Presidency was the Vietnam War. He inherited the policy of containment from which it sprang and the agenda of the Kennedy Administration which tried to prevent what was believed to be the next soft point for communist aggression. Chinese communists were thought to be as threatening as Soviet communists. They governed China, having overthrown Chiang Kai-Shek and his nationalist government in the late 1940s.

Johnson and his Cabinet leaders, including Robert McNamara, Secretary of Defense, decided in 1965 that the best course of action was to substantially increase troop levels in Vietnam and defeat the Viet Cong, restore order and return power to the government in Saigon and President Diem. That the judgments of the American government were badly mistaken was finally and honestly stated by Robert McNamara years after American troops were out of the country. He said "We were wrong" and reiterated his point in anguished words.[7] Specifically, the misjudgments were about the intentions of the North Vietnamese and their guerilla warriors, the Viet Cong, particularly, when the war escalated with the sending of more troops, and then later more troops. Johnson himself was alarmed at the thought that communism was making advances anywhere in the world. His roots were in Texas, a State that was particularly affected by the McCarthy charges about communism in government. And then a few communists were found in government. He told his aides that the Russians were not to be trusted.[8]

David Halberstam wrote his book *The Best And The Brightest* after exhaustive research and interviews with several hundred people who had served in government in the 1960s. His book is about how the best and brightest people in the country were attracted to the young President elected in 1960, and agreed to serve in that government. Kennedy selected some whom he knew and some whose credentials from the best universities, business and industry recommended them for cabinet positions and advisory posts in the White House. People like McGeorge Bundy, Robert McNamara from General Motors, known for his systems management expertise, for Secretary of Defense, Dean Rusk for Secretary of State, and his own brother Robert Kennedy for Attorney General. The pleasant myth of Camelot surrounded this Presidency. So, Halberstam's question was how could these smart, well-endowed best people bring the country to the disaster of Vietnam?

Lyndon Johnson was elected overwhelmingly in 1964, a year after the Kennedy assassination, with the recent passage of the Civil Rights Act to his credit and with a campaign promise to not allow a "land war in Asia." But in the spring of 1965, things looked different. By 1965 there were misunderstandings and misperceptions about the war, the worst being that there was no specific objective for that war. What was the mission? Was it to drive the communists out of North Vietnam? Or was it only to stop the communists from taking over the country? The answer, explained General Wheeler to the President, would dictate how many troops should be sent and how the war should be managed.[9] McGeorge Bundy, in a speech to the Council on Foreign Relations, told his listeners that in White House discussions there was a "'premium on imprecision' and the political and military leaders did not speak candidly to each other."[10] Bundy was saying, in effect, that if the leaders had faced the situation candidly about the cost of the war and the length of it, they would not have formed a consensus around the President's wishes. "The men around Johnson served him poorly, but they served him poorly because he wanted them to." Only Clark Clifford objected, saying that the North Vietnamese would send more of their troops if we sent more of ours.[11] Moreover, the Chinese would send their troops. There would be no end to the escalation. He declared in a meeting that "'I see catastrophe ahead for my country.'"[12]

The President placed a priority on his Great Society programs. He wanted to see Congress act on his initiatives. While the war was not secondary to that, he did believe that Vietnam was a fourth-rate country that could easily be straightened out and the North Vietnamese beaten. The question was simply what strategy would work. Johnson, however, knew he had won the election in 1964 by assuring the public that he would not send large numbers of American troops to Asia. When in 1965, he concluded it was necessary to increase dramatically the number of troops in Vietnam, he didn't make any public statements to that fact and gave the press to believe that a small number of additional troops were needed.[13]

The Joint Chiefs of Staff foresaw a very tough war, very expensive, costly in terms of troops and likely to take maybe 6 or 7 years. They thought that government should go on a wartime footing and call up the reserves as well. A wartime footing involved budgeting for a war that would send in many more troops than the initial 50,000 that the President had decided to dispatch, hoping it would not look like too much of an escalation. In time, of course, a major escalation took place in the effort to put an end to what was perceived to be the communist threat in Vietnam. The number being bandied about the

White House in 1965-66 was 300,000. As for how it could happen, there were several serious mistakes: lack of precision as to what the mission was, deliberate efforts to conceal how badly the war was going, and a false consensus among those who made the decisions. Fifty-two thousand American troops were killed in the war.

Societal Stresses

Senator Fulbright's Committee investigating the conduct of the war, the growing restiveness in the nation about a host of ills, the intensifying civil rights movement with charges of discrimination in schools, housing, and jobs, kept government officers scrambling to right wrongs. Long hot summers with cities burning while protests against the war became unmanageable were the prospects that Lyndon Johnson confronted. So in March, 1968, he declared that he would not run for the Presidency again. He took steps to bring about a truce in Vietnam which would involve a negotiation with the North Vietnamese government.

While the activists opposed the Vietnam War and carried on their demonstrations in Washington and elsewhere, they also carried their impassioned insistence on the correction of racial injustice to all corners of the country. The public endured the burning of cities, the dominance of the youth culture, dominant because there were so many of them, and the assassinations of two prominent figures in 1968, Martin Luther King and Robert Kennedy. And while there was much appeal to peace, and getting out of the war, there did not seem to be much peace where activists were able to attract the news media.

Lyndon Johnson lost support of the people in part because he did not communicate well publicly. But he got some valuable programs going, all designed to meet the needs of the poor and to build the economy. By one study of Presidents and the American economy, Johnson ranked as the best manager of it.[14] The Vietnam War was what hurt his presidency. He was trying to end it through negotiations in Paris, but the outcry generally in this country was about many other things, including a generation growing up, and he decided in March of 1968 that he could not serve the nation further. In many ways he had been very successful. The Great Society programs were functioning to the benefit of many people. Johnson brought a costly railroad strike to an end. He negotiated with business leaders for the benefit of the economy. In the end, however, he believed he should step aside for the good of the country.

RICHARD MILHOUS NIXON

1969-1974

In spite of the wrongs committed by Richard Nixon, hurting himself and others in the White House, he also served the country's best interests in his five years as President, making progress in key foreign policy initiatives. He opened the door to new relationships with China intended to bring that country of 800 million people out of isolation and into the community of nations. He achieved progress in U.S.-Soviet relations after much tedious negotiation, and finally he held three summit meetings with Leonid Brezhnev which had lasting benefits for both nations. He presided over the negotiated settlement with North Vietnam which was carried out mainly by Henry Kissinger, his National Security Adviser, who handled the negotiations for all three foreign policy successes. Finally, Nixon supported the Comprehensive Nuclear Non-Proliferation Treaty which President Johnson had signed and sent to the Senate for ratification. It was ratified and went into force in March, 1970. This Treaty was the product of years of negotiation among nuclear powers and non-nuclear powers in the United Nations.

However, from a democratic perspective there were dangerous flaws in his governing principles. His need to control events, and especially the war in Vietnam, led him to a number of actions that have been questioned by historians and legal scholars. His order to invade Cambodia was a case in point. He justified his action of invading a neutral state by saying that he had to protect American fighting men in Vietnam. He said that he had the power to do this as part of the President's war power – as Commander in Chief of the military forces. But Nixon, and Lyndon Johnson before him, stretched the war power, in the words of Arthur Schlesinger, Jr.[1] Nixon acted without consulting Congress and in some of his actions he scarcely consulted the State Department. Concerning Cambodia, there was not a real national emergency that threatened the United States. Congress had not been consulted nor was the United Nations involved. The various opinions regarding the war power may or may not include a President's need to control his foreign policy, but what is clear is that if a President feels this need he probably will act on it. Asking Congress for authority to take the action he thinks necessary would at least legitimize it and this Nixon did not do in the case of Cambodia.

Richard Nixon was born in Yorba Linda, California, where his father owned a small lemon farm. Richard was a good student; graduated from Whittier College and took his law degree at Duke University Law School, intending to practice law. He joined a law firm in Whittier, but in 1937 he moved to Washington and got a job in the Office of Price Administration, his first real exposure to the federal government. He joined the Navy in 1942, received the rank of lieutenant and served as an operations officer with the South Pacific Combat Air Transport Command during the Second World War. After the War, he ran for Congress as a Republican and was elected in 1946 on a platform that urged a return to free enterprise. He argued that the Democrats opposed the free enterprise system, an argument that had currency in the 1940s after years of New Deal legislation that introduced regulations of many businesses in the country, including significant regulations in agriculture.

The Congressman was appointed to the House Un-American Activities Committee, which investigated the entertainment industry. The Committee blacklisted 320 artists in the movie industry and elsewhere by the time it was finished its investigations. Much of this was done because the FBI's J. Edgar Hoover supplied the Committee Chairman, Richard Nixon, with information about Communist Party memberships of a number of these people. The interrogations of such people as Elizabeth Bentley and Whittaker Chambers led to the prosecution of Alger Hiss, Harry Gold, David Greenglass, and Ethel and Julius Rosenberg. Of that group, only the Rosenbergs were found guilty of activities that were treasonous. They were executed. They were responsible for providing the Soviet Union with information about the development of the atomic bomb and the continuing work at Los Alamos, New Mexico. Hiss had been a government official in the State Department, had been sympathetic to liberal causes and possibly communist ideas, but he was not a traitor. He was accused by Whittaker Chambers of membership in the Communist Party. Chambers was himself a member of the Communist Party who left it in 1937.[2]

Nixon was chosen to run on the Republican ticket for Vice-President in 1952, with Dwight Eisenhower running for President. They were elected, the popular Eisenhower drawing strong support from a people who wanted the United States to end the war in Korea. Ike promised to go to Korea if elected. In 1956, they were re-elected; Nixon thus had eight years of experience in the White House and could reasonably aspire to becoming President in the future.

He ran for the office in 1960 and in a very close race against John Kennedy he was defeated. Returning to California, he ran for Governor in 1962, but again lost his bid. At that point, feeling embittered, he retired to private law practice at home. However, politics was forever in his system, and even though he found it hard to function as a glad-handing candidate, he worked to overcome that handicap. He simply forced himself to appear warm and engaging.

Nixon was elected President with his running mate Spiro Agnew in November, 1968. They defeated the popular Vice-President Hubert Humphrey. In his inaugural speech, Nixon urged that "we lower our voices." His plate was full with serious problems: the by now extremely unpopular war in Vietnam, the detritus of burned cities in his own country and a disaffected public that wanted only peace. He was a master of organization but his skill at this led him to try to over-control the government organization.[3] He used various devices of control which were not popular with some of his advisers and staff. He would go around a subordinate or leave one out of a conversation that involved that person's portfolio. He would ignore an inconvenient contact when it might get in the way of his control over the administration of a program. He has been correctly described as a man who felt he was inadequate, a feeling that is common among leaders in a variety of careers not only in America but in any nation at any time in history.

Richard Nixon had a complex personality, according to those who knew him well. He was intelligent, had a quick grasp of difficult situations, and had learned much about the workings of government from his years as Vice-President of the United States. However, he was awkward socially, and suspicious of others. In order to run for election he trained himself and required of himself the visible signs of camaraderie, friendliness and what he thought were the social graces. But these gestures often were visibly false, and sometimes he had trouble appearing to be sincere.[4] He did not trust some people with whom he worked. He did not trust the bureaucracy in place when he came into office, the permanent civil service employees in the departments and agencies of government.

For example, according to Henry Kissinger in his book of memoirs, Nixon appointed William Rogers to be Secretary of State but did not want him to control foreign policy.[5] Rather, he leaned on his National Security Adviser, Kissinger, to conduct many foreign policy negotiations for him, particularly in those three areas of greatest concern to the President, the Soviet Union, China, and Vietnam. Nixon was secretive and circuitous in his dealings with people, both inside and outside government.

Nixon was born into a family of very limited means and seemed to always think of himself as not able to measure up to people of means and power. Privately, he played his piano, enjoyed his family and was tender toward his children. He was a sensitive man, often finding it painfully difficult to meet someone new to him and engage in important discussion. Yet he exhibited sensitivity toward Chou En Lai and Mao Tse Tung in China, and apparently had learned to deal with honored guests at formal dinners with the Prime Minister of Great Britain. It may be that some years after his resignation and the inevitable shame that brought to him, he was finally able to accept himself. One would not know from his *Memoirs* that he was so shy, dreading social relationships. The *Memoirs* are an invaluable resource in studying his work and experience in government.

Nixon had an excellent National Security Adviser in Kissinger, and much was accomplished in foreign policy because of him. The settlement of the Vietnam War, the visit to China, the planned summit meetings and SALT talks with the Soviets, and the efforts to resolve the continuing Mideast crisis, mainly between Israel and the Palestinians were all managed by Kissinger.

Much other work was accomplished by the Nixon Administration, in dealing with the economy, in dealing with the dissidents in American society who were setting fires in the cities, creating a threatening atmosphere in public meetings, especially political meetings and rallies. On one occasion at a public meeting in San Jose, California, where Nixon was campaigning for members of Congress in 1970, he was physically attacked by a mob throwing rocks, eggs and whatever was handy. The Secret Service hustled him into a car and he was whisked away.[6]

The Economy

The Nixon Administration had to deal with a variable economy. The President decided that the country needed to improve its balance of trade with foreign countries; to make this happen, Nixon removed the U.S. from the gold standard set in the Bretton Woods agreement.[7] Instead of having foreign currencies pegged to the U.S. dollar, exchange rates should float, he argued. He looked for more exports to bring in income to the nation and reduce imports which caused money to go the other way. This policy worked for a time, but in spite of all efforts by his Administration he was unable to stem the inflation rate.

Seldom, if ever, does the American economic system settle into a smooth process of buying and selling, whether on a small scale or a large scale. The free enterprise system tends to keep it this way, with times of relative prosperity and times of economic decline. In the final analysis, the government does not completely control the economy; through the President and the Fed, it manages it. It seems as if government, whether Republican or Democratic, has to busy itself with adjusting and readjusting its tools of fiscal controls and monetary controls to maintain a rough balance of economic measures.

In his Memoirs Nixon discussed the views of previous Presidents about the role of the government in the economy, and in so doing he referred to the views of several scholars and Presidents on the subject. They had concluded that there were phases of action and periods of conservatism about government action. These phases occurred about every 30 years of so. If this was true, the United States had just gone through an active phase with the new programs generated by the Johnson administration.[8]

In the Nixon years, there was serious concern about unemployment, which had reached 6% nation-wide. There were also inflation and high prices, conditions that meant that increasing numbers of people fell into poverty. Nixon believed that the Johnson Administration's Great Society programs were very wrong for the country. They were financed by deficit spending. However, Nixon could not begin to dismantle these programs, he could only begin to reduce the financial commitments made to them in the Federal budget. Conscious of the loss of confidence reflected in the stock market, and listening to his advisers and to members of Congress, Nixon reluctantly set up a program of mandatory but temporary wage and price controls in August, 1971. These controls were designed to function in several phases so that in two and one-half years they would finally be lifted.[9] The action was very popular at first, but when controls were phased out in 1974, inflation returned, and there were energy shortages and high prices for food.[10]

The Nixon Administration also reduced income taxes, which had the effect of removing low-income people from the tax rolls entirely. Production controls were removed from agriculture, and the Administration took the lead in setting up a worldwide system of free exchange rates. Promoting negotiations to remove trade barriers was an important long-range achievement.[11]

Foreign Policy

The diplomatic approach to China had gained currency among the Eastern internationalist group of Republicans in the '60s. Nixon wrote an article for *Foreign Affairs* in which he wrote,

> Taking the long view, we simply cannot afford to leave China forever outside the family of nations, there to nurture its fantasies, cherish its hates and threaten its neighbors. . . For the short run, then, this means a policy of firm restraint, of no reward, of creative counterpressure designed to persuade Peking that its interests can be served only by accepting the basic rules of international civility. For the long run, it means pulling China back into the world community – but as a great and progressing nation, not as the epicenter of world revolution.[12]

President Nixon meets with China's Communist Party Leader,
Mao Tse-Tung, 02/29/1972
Source: Nixon Presidential Materials, U.S. National Archives
Author: White House Photo Office (1969-1974)

Kissinger himself thought it would be beneficial to create a triangular relationship between Washington, Moscow and Peking that could "give us a great strategic opportunity for peace."[13] Both he and Nixon perceived that the United States needed help from Moscow and Peking to bring about a settlement with North Vietnam. Nelson Rockefeller, then Governor of New York and a close friend of Kissinger, said in a speech in July, 1968,

> We will have to learn to deal imaginatively with several competing centers of Communist power. . . I would begin a dialogue with Communist China. In a subtle triangle of relations between Washington, Peking, and Moscow, we improve the possibilities of accommodations with each as we increase our options toward both.[14]

Nixon's major achievements were his substantive meetings with the Soviets, mainly Kosygin and Brezhnev, the Ambassador to the U.S. and the Chairman of the Communist Party, respectively, and the opening of negotiations with China which led to lessening of tensions between the two nations. With the Soviets, the goals were to complete strategic arms limitation agreements, the SALT negotiations and settlement. With China, just opening the door to improved relationships was the objective. Nixon believed that in the long run the tremendous energy, strength and discipline of the Chinese people would place them in a leading role among nations, and friendly relationships were essential between the United States and China. Nixon's third major achievement was the ending of the war in Vietnam. But Nixon saw the three issues as inter-related; it would be necessary to persuade the Soviets of that. In his *Memoirs*, Nixon wrote,

> During the transition period (after the 1968 election) Kissinger and I developed a new policy for dealing with the Soviets. Since the U.S.-Soviet interests as the world's two competing nuclear superpowers were so widespread and overlapping, it was unrealistic to separate or compartmentalize areas of concern. Therefore we decided to link progress in such areas of concern as strategic arms limitation and increased trade with progress in areas that were important to us – Vietnam, the Mideast, and Berlin. This concept became known as linkage....

> Linkage was something uncomfortably new and different for the Soviets, and I was not surprised when they bridled at the restraints it imposed on our relationship. It would take almost two years of patient and hard-nosed determination on our part before they would accept that linkage with what we wanted from them was the price they would have to pay for getting any of the things they wanted from us.[15]

Nixon had promised the public in 1968 that he would negotiate an end to the Vietnam War, and he struggled with this for almost four years. In the delicate maneuvering of international diplomacy, the concerned parties were not in agreement. Kissinger continued his patient discussions with the North Vietnamese, represented by Le Duc Tho, while the South Vietnamese President Thieu held out for a settlement that required Hanoi to agree formally to remove its troops. By late 1972, Kissinger was close to a settlement with Hanoi but then they stepped back and would not agree to remove their troops from the South. The South Vietnamese government feared that the withdrawal of American troops would leave it vulnerable to renewed fighting and ultimately the loss of its war with the North.

To encourage the North to agree to remove their troops from the South, Nixon ordered an intense bombing of Hanoi and Haiphong, the most devastating bombing that had ever occurred in world history. Kissinger wrote in his *White House Years* that President Nixon was inclined to go for the jugular toward an enemy when he thought it necessary. The intensive bombing illustrated that tendency, but it did bring the desired result. Meanwhile, the U.S. Congress was restive and unhappy that the negotiations took so long and seemed to be so inconclusive. They were appalled when Nixon ordered that intensive bombing campaign on December 18, 1972. In 1973, two committees of Congress reached a decision that the war in Cambodia should be ended and no more funds should be allowed for combat activities. Nixon vetoed the bill, but knowing that further legislation would be introduced to accomplish the same thing, he and committee leaders in the Congress agreed to a cut-off date of August 15, 1973. In November, 1973, Congress passed the War Powers Act. Both of these actions, in Nixon's view, weakened the position of his Administration with regard to Vietnam and Cambodia.[16]

While the President had used the intensive bombing to bring the North Vietnamese to an agreement, he also wanted to demonstrate good faith with the South Vietnamese who were not anxious for a peace settlement unless it would secure the South's government. Kissinger himself had reservations about the intensive bombing, but he later told Nixon that it had been a courageous act and had brought about the desired result in a very difficult situation. Nixon said in his *Memoirs,*

> Reporting afterward, Kissinger said that the South Vietnamese leaders exhibited a surprising awe of Communist cunning and a disquieting lack of confidence in themselves. It was clear that they were having great psychological difficulty with the prospect of cutting the American umbilical cord. As Kissinger saw the situation, we were up against a paradoxical situation in which North Vietnam, which had in effect lost the war, was acting as if it had won; while South Vietnam, which had effectively won the war, was acting as if it had lost.[17]

In October, 1972, the North and the South agreed to create a National Council of Reconciliation and Concord made up of representatives of the government, the Vietcong, and neutral members.[18] This would be a substitute for a coalition government which the North had been demanding. The North would receive economic aid from the U.S. and they would stop demanding that President Thieu resign. There remained the issue of the release of Vietnamese civilian prisoners and several other matters that had to be resolved, but Nixon and Kissinger were celebrating an agreement in the Fall for a cease fire by the end of October, believing that the smaller details would be worked out. By December, it was clear that they would not; the North was refusing to agree to remove their troops from the South as part of a settlement. President Thieu also was reluctant to agree to the settlement. Nixon then ordered the intensive bombing of Haiphong.

When he was re-elected in November, 1972, Nixon hoped to finish the negotiations by the end of his first term. The frustrating course of negotiations continued. But on January 9, Kissinger was able to cable Nixon that the North had agreed to the terms the President wanted. By the end of the month, signatures had been accomplished and the war had ended. The subsequent chaotic withdrawal of the Americans from Vietnam was a cause of much grief in the United States. Henry Kissinger thought the withdrawal was so chaotic because effective leadership in America was absent at that critical time. The reason: Watergate.[19]

When Nixon looked at the prospects for being re-elected in 1972 he picked out a few danger signs. One was a possible news item that had bedeviled his political career before. Nixon suspected that Larry O'Brien was working as a lobbyist for Howard Hughes at the same time that he was Chairman of the Democratic National Committee, a conflict of interest. He wanted proof of that to protect himself from another possible attack by O'Brien because, in the 1950s, Nixon's brother Don had received a large loan from Hughes and this information appeared in the press just before the 1960 presidential election.[20] Nixon thought that news item had contributed to his loss in the election to Kennedy, a race that was very close. Then in 1962, when Nixon ran for governor of California, that news item appeared again, and Nixon was defeated by Pat Brown. Nixon suspected that the same story would reappear during his campaign for the presidency in 1972 (apparently, it didn't) and he wanted to neutralize it before it happened. He needed to discover whether Larry O'Brien was a lobbyist for Howard Hughes at the same time that he was Chairman of the Democratic National Committee. Such a news item would certainly embarrass O'Brien and the Democratic Committee too.

The way to get the information Nixon wanted was to tap O'Brien's telephone and at the same time have an eavesdropping device in the office of the Democratic National Committee at the Watergate apartment complex. A burglary would have to be arranged to get in and place the devices. Nixon discussed this with H.R. Haldeman, one of his close advisers. Haldeman years later said he thought the plan was absurd, but that Nixon seemed fixated on Hughes. It turned out that in 1976, several years after the event,

Haldeman, in a discussion with Nixon, learned that a prospective campaign contribution of $100,000 that was never delivered to the (Democratic) Campaign Committee was sitting in the safe deposit box of Bebe Rebozo, Nixon's close friend.[21] This may answer the question why a President with several successes accomplished would risk a stupid (Nixon's word) burglary out of fear of not getting re-elected. His record as President was strong and positive.

Dealing With the Soviet Union

U-2 reconnaissance flights over Cuba revealed in September, 1970, that the Soviets were constructing a submarine base in Cienfuegos Bay. The Administration believed that this would be a base for nuclear weapons-bearing subs.[22] The previous agreement between Krhushchev and Kennedy in 1962 had included the statement that the Soviets would not put offensive, particularly nuclear weapons, in Cuba. So now, in 1970, Nixon and Kissinger wanted to pressure the Soviets to stop that suspicious construction and to prevent the information about it from becoming a public cause for panic among Americans. Their strategy worked.

Nixon and Kissinger decided to keep it as quiet as possible; meanwhile Kissinger in a meeting with Soviet Ambassador Anatoly Dobrynin let on that he was concerned about an upcoming summit meeting with Brezhnev. Dobrynin told Kissinger that his government also wanted a summit meeting with Nixon, but he did not mention the sub base. Unfortunately, word about it had been leaked by some Deputy Assistant Secretary in the Defense Department. Kissinger talked about dates for the summit meeting, never mentioning to Dobrynin anything about the base. Kissinger had to talk to reporters once the news was out, but he did so by saying that we didn't know whether the story about the base was true or not.

Kissinger told Dobrynin that the Administration knew exactly what was going on in Cuba but would hold off letting the American people know about it so that the Soviets would have time to change their position.[23] They did so. Nixon in his *Memoirs* crowed a bit about this, believing that the American people were spared a bad scare like the one they had in 1962.[24] Meanwhile, Dobrynin and the Soviets accepted the dates for a summit with Nixon.

Kissinger made a preliminary visit to China as part of the preparation for Nixon's visit, which the Chinese leaders had agreed to. When the President went to China in 1972, he and his hosts found agreeable things to talk about, including the desire that both nations had for peace. They wanted to promote trade with each other. Nixon extended a warm invitation to Chou En Lai to come to Washington.

Meanwhile, in the Western Hemisphere, Chile elected its new President, Salvadore Allende in 1970. Believing that Allende was a possible threat to the hemisphere, President Nixon ordered the CIA to support the opponents of Allende and work to prevent his election. Kennedy and Johnson had done this in their turn, but now, because Allende had received such a small plurality in the popular election, he had to be elected by the Chilean Congress. He was overthrown by the Chilean military in 1973, however, because of a failing economy and crippling strikes.[25]

The Nixon administration eliminated the draft, and instituted the volunteer army in January, 1973. This was actually an economy move, taken when a number of costs the government had to deal with were under consideration, but it was very popular as an alternative to the hated draft.

There were three summit meetings between Nixon and Brezhnev in 1972 -1974. The first was in Moscow where the two and their staffs agreed to limit strategic arms, which was included in the Interim Agreement. The Anti-Ballistic Missile treaty would put an end to a defensive arms race which was under way at the time. It would also introduce the concept of deterrence through mutually-assured destruction, as it was later described. In addition to these agreements, several other important agreements were reached: the means for the reduction of tensions and conflict, a joint commission on commercial matters to encourage trade, and on pollution control and research on public health.[26]

The second summit was held in June, 1973 in Washington. The Soviets wanted to get the US to agree by treaty to not use nuclear weapons. Nixon and Kissinger explained that that would confuse our European allies. Kissinger then drafted a proposal that both Nixon and Brezhnev could accept: the two countries agreed not to use force against each other and between the US and third countries. The two principals signed that agreement. Discussions on SALT continued. A final matter was the concern of the Russians about Soviet Jews who were not allowed to emigrate from the Soviet Union.[27] The Russians wanted Most Favored Nation status with the United States which would improve trade between the two countries. Nixon asked Congress for the authority to extend MFN status to the Soviet Union, but some months after the second summit, it was rejected by Congress. The summit discussions and agreements had proceeded in June, 1973 with Brezhnev, Dobrynin attending. Stressing the desire of all Americans for a peaceful relationship with the Soviet Union, Nixon took Brezhnev to San Clemente where he stayed for a couple of days. Finally, Nixon gave him a Lincoln Continental, donated by the manufacturer.[28]

The third summit was held in July 1974 in Moscow, a month before Nixon resigned the Presidency. At this meeting, Nixon said that they should try to complete a SALT accord before the end of the year. Anti-ballistic missiles should be limited to one site, and underground tests should also be limited.

Richard Nixon was as close as anyone can be to impeachment in 1974, but he resigned before it could happen. He had allowed his suspicions to carry him too far, to the point that he had an enemies list, had instructed a subordinate to stop the leaks that were endemic to the White House in the 1960s and early 1970s. There were others, so-called Plumbers, who were told to plug leaks and report their sources. In a sense Nixon was hoist on his own petard. Having developed an active suspicion of people in the White House and outside it, his behavior led people to suspect him of many things. Nevertheless, his White House, like that of Lyndon Johnson, had tried to cope with a nation in a revolution. Both of them decided that they could not do the good they wanted to do for the nation any longer. Johnson declared that he would not be a candidate in 1968 and Nixon resigned rather than try to defend himself in 1974. But his work in his years as President was good work: the reaching out to China, the resolving of strains between the US and the USSR, not to mention the peace agreement with North Vietnam, were all work that cried out for attention, and he with Kissinger acted positively to settle them for the benefit of the US and the world.

Kissinger thought the nation had a spiritual void related to the managerial and consumer-oriented society it had become.[29] He thought that Nixon brought the nation through dangerous times with success.

What extraordinary vehicles destiny selects to accomplish its design. This man, so lonely in his hour of triumph, so ungenerous in some of his motivations, had navigated our nation through one of the most anguishing periods in its history. Not by nature courageous, he had steeled himself to conspicuous acts of rare courage. Not normally outgoing, he had forced himself to rally his people to its challenge. He had striven for revolution in American foreign policy so that it would overcome the disastrous oscillations between overcommitment and isolation. Despised by the Establishment, ambiguous in his human perceptions, he had yet held fast to a sense of national honor and responsibility, determined to prove that the strongest free country had no right to abdicate.[30]

GERALD R. FORD

1974-1977

After Nixon flew away to San Clemente, the new President, Gerald Ford, rose from the Vice Presidency to the highest office in the land. He had several challenges before him, particularly the domestic situation, still roiling after Nixon's departure. President Ford did not have a clear plan to deal with it because he hoped that the nation's leaders, both in Congress and in the government, would see the need for a restoration of domestic peace. When it did not, he took a very courageous step; he issued a full pardon for Richard Nixon, not to relieve the former President of further legal action against him that surely would have followed his departure, but to bring peace to the country. He thought that the only way to put an end to recriminations and further charges and counter-charges was to put an end to legal action of any kind concerning Watergate. Ford did not expect an agreeable reception to his decision, and there were those who disapproved of his action. But gradually, by changing the subject, he brought people back to focus on the present problems of inflation and petroleum shortages.

GERALD R. FORD
This file is from Wikipedia Commons

Ford appointed Nelson Rockefeller to be Vice President. He worked to reduce regulatory restrictions on American businesses, and to reduce taxes. He continued the Nixon policies in Southeast Asia by dealing with the collapse of South Vietnam and Cambodia.

The President had several economic problems on his plate when he took office in August 1944, the continuing problem of inflation, and gasoline shortages. Within a month or two after he became President, he made an appeal to the public and to Congress to begin a program he called WIN: Whip Inflation Now. The shortness of his term in office put a damper on this effort.

Ford was highly respected by his fellow Congressmen and Senators and then by the nation for his service as President. He lost the election of 1976 to Jimmy Carter, but it was a narrow victory for Carter, and in the ensuing years Ford and Carter became the best of friends.

JAMES EARL CARTER, JR.

1977-1981

Jimmy Carter served one term as President, and had it not been for the capture of some 50 Americans by the Iranians who kept them as hostages, he probably would have been re-elected in 1980. He accomplished a great deal in his four years as President.

Jimmy Carter was raised in Archery, near Plains, Georgia, and went to school there as his family lived and worked on a farm. As a young man he entered the Naval Academy and after graduation as a young naval officer he worked with Admiral Rickover on the design and other features of a nuclear submarine. After about six years in the Navy, he decided that he wanted to resign and go home with his wife Rosalynn to Plains to live. Back in Georgia, he went into business and became interested in politics. He ran for the State Senate and later was elected Governor of Georgia. He served a term as Governor before preparing the groundwork for a run for President in 1976. He was nominated for President by the Democratic Party and won the election against Ford. He was the classic "dark horse" candidate, the product of a modest background not known outside of Georgia. In many ways, he personified the South. He is a deeply religious man but does not broadcast his faith.

Early in his life Carter became fascinated with the Holy Land, so much a part of his religious heritage. This deep interest remained a strong force throughout his life. So it is not surprising that Israel and its Middle East neighbors became the locus of his greatest foreign policy achievement, the peace treaty agreed to by Menachem Begin, Prime Minister of Israel and Anwar Sadat, President of Egypt. Now at 84, Carter continues to travel in behalf of the Carter Center which provides funds contributed for its purposes of promoting peace, health, and hope around the world. While many of its resources go to Africa and South America, the Middle East has been a focus for the peace efforts of the Center.

Carter and his Administration tackled the problems in the economy – inflation and unemployment – and after four years his efforts and those of his Administration produced 8 million new jobs, even though inflation continued. A short recession appeared to have been caused by efforts to reduce interest rates. He was committed to a balanced budget policy, and he hoped his Administration could carry out the plan recommended by his transition team. His budgets did result in a decrease in the budget deficit, but the expectation was that the gross national product would be about five-and-a-half to six percent annually. It did not perform that well, and the deficit remained.[1]

Carter had managed a government reorganization of the State government of Georgia, and he wanted to apply what he had learned to the federal bureaucracy. He proposed eleven reorganization plans of which ten were accepted by Congress under a "reverse legislation" policy. That policy allowed a proposed reorganization plan to become law unless House or Senate rejected it.[2]

He proposed a national energy policy which included the decontrol of domestic gasoline prices. He made a major effort to tackle the growing demand for oil products in the country, trying to alert the people to the dangers of becoming too dependent on foreign sources of oil. He was much concerned about the threat to the national security that this dependence involved. He demonstrated what needed to be done by having the thermostats in the White House and federal buildings turned down and by holding a televised fireside chat with the people dressed in a cardigan sweater. He explained that in the previous four years before he took office, this country's dependence on imported oil had risen from 35% to 50%. The public was well aware of the problem after the oil shocks of 1973 and 1975, but resisted changing its habits. In the end, he was able to create a cabinet Department of Energy and appoint a Secretary of Energy, James Schlesinger. While the House of Representatives passed his omnibus energy plan, it died in the Senate where industry lobbyists were very active.[3] Twenty-five years later, Americans were paying the price.

Carter's other achievements included the deregulation of the trucking, rail and airline industries. He appointed a number of women, blacks and Hispanics to government jobs. His Administration set up the Department of Education. He completed the SALT II treaty which placed limits on the numbers of offensive strategic arms the United States and the Soviet Union had at the time of treaty signing, in 1979, and agreed to not increase them.[4] Carter announced the formal recognition of China beginning in 1979. While the initial hard work on this was done by Nixon and Kissinger, the matter had to be finalized and Carter was glad to do it. He pressed human rights issues in other nations. The Camp David agreement between Egypt and Israel still survives. He also persuaded the Senate to ratify the Panama Canal treaties.

Congress assigned to the State Department the task of preparing reports about human rights in other nations as a basis for providing American financial and other assistance to them. The reports are made to Congress. In later years, this was seen as American paternalism by friends and enemies abroad.

Jimmy Carter's proudest achievement was the Camp David Accords between Egypt and Israel. This agreement is still observed thirty years later. After he took office in 1977, Carter began this foreign policy initiative to bring about peace between Egypt and Israel. Following the Yom Kippur War in 1973, Henry Kissinger had conducted a shuttle diplomacy between the countries in an effort to gain peace in a step-by-step fashion. Such negotiations are sometimes frustrating and seem to be unending. Carter wanted to try a more comprehensive approach, involving a calling together of the participants in the Geneva Conference of 1973, which would include a Palestinian delegation. President Carter met with Anwar Sadat, Yitzhak Rabin of Israel, King Hussein of Jordan and Hafez al-Assad of Syria as part of his own preparation for establishing the groundwork for future negotiations. Those meetings produced little, but Carter and Zbigniev Brzezinski, his national security advisor, went ahead with planning a meeting between Sadat and Menachem Begin, Prime Minister of Israel.[5]

Anwar Sadat went personally to Israel to meet with Begin, having first sounded him out privately. Sadat, by making this trip was in effect recognizing Israel, the first Arab nation to do so. He used the opportunity to address the Knesset where he talked about the status of Israel's occupied territories and the Palestinian refugees. He discussed the importance of peace. There was a good deal of hostility toward Egypt all around the Middle East and even among some of the Warsaw Pact countries still supporting the Soviet cause. They threatened to attack Egypt if it made a peace agreement with Israel and if it did not revoke its recognition of Israel. Both Sadat and Begin, however, saw benefits to talking about an agreement, for Egypt economic aid from the United States and for Israel the opportunity to deal only with Egypt rather than with other Arab countries together which would be likely to make demands Israel could not accept.

President Carter with Sadat and Begin
Place: White House lawn
Date: March 16, 1979
Credit: The Jimmy Carter Library

The peace agreement between Egypt and Israel was worked out at Camp David in September, 1978, the President facilitating the negotiations. The atmosphere was tense. President Carter was unrelenting in his insistence that they not leave until they had an agreement. The two parties disliked each other and would not meet in person, so Carter went back and forth between them for 13 days until it was done. The Accords established a framework for negotiations to establish a self-governing authority in the West Bank and Gaza, a basis for a peace treaty concerning the future of Sinai, and a promise by the United States to provide several billion dollars worth of economic aid to both countries each year. This aid continues to the present day. When it was settled, Carter invited Sadat and Begin to the White House where their agreement was made public. President Carter received the Nobel Peace Prize in 2003 for his work in this negotiation and for his establishment of the Carter Center dedicated to peace after his Presidency.[6]

Carter was nominated again for President by the Democrats in 1980, but he and Walter Mondale did not win against the popular Ronald Reagan. The seizure by Iran of 52 Americans in Teheran the year before, and Carter's inability to gain their release, was the primary reason for his loss in the election. There were other reasons too. He was perceived by people as being unable to exert leadership with Congress. Some people thought him too moralistic. But the hostage crisis was the ultimate problem.

He and Rosalynn went back to Plains, Georgia, and in a year or two established the Carter Center in Atlanta whose chosen work is to eradicate disease, promote peace around the world, and give hope to its vast numbers of destitute people. It is fair to say that Carter simply continued his foreign policy through this means. He has been able to raise funds for the Center's work, and its benefits are measurable in Africa where serious endemic illnesses like guinea worm disease have been all but eliminated by the work of this philanthropic agency.

RONALD WILSON REAGAN
1981-1989

Ronald Reagan was an artist. An actor by profession, he knew that appearances can be seen as the real thing. He knew how to create appearances that become real in the public's mind. Moreover, an important part of his communication with the public was his deep love of America.

The collapse of the communist experiment in the Soviet Union just as Reagan was ending his second term gave this nation a large dose of optimism looking toward a world at peace.

What Reagan did superbly well was to give Americans confidence in themselves and the nation. He personified what Americans most wanted at that time, a leader who could articulate an American dream. The dream came out of the movies, in fact, a vision of a strong, good man, athletic, law-abiding. A man who took a bullet near his heart and recovered heroically. In fact, his physical strength was what saved him. In his teens Reagan was a lifeguard at a local swimming pool in Dixon, Illinois, his home town. He played football in college. He rode horseback most of his life. As a septuagenarian he still chopped wood at his ranch in California, even after he had recovered from the gunshot wound in 1981.

The Economy

What was the Reagan Revolution? It was a restatement of the American myth, that hard work will bring a person wealth, that America was better than other countries, and protected by God. Individual enterprise would advance the nation, government should let a man's initiative carry him as far as it can. Adam Smith's ideas were resuscitated. There was also an unspoken element of Social Darwinism in this myth. Government should not make transfer payments to the people who did not work, for whatever reason. Poor people were poor because they didn't want to work. It was up to them to make their own way. The Council of Economic Advisers wrote in its 1982 annual report,

> (C)ash transfers to the poor interfere with the workings of the private marketplace and weaken the national economy. . . 'Transfers reduce the incentive of recipients to work and taxes imposed on the rest of society to finance those transfers also cause losses in efficiency.'"[1]

Although the Carter Administration had struggled with inflation and a recession, the costs to run the government continued to remain high. In the Reagan years, a budget deficit was an annual condition. David Stockman, Reagan's Budget Director, began to use the deficit to accomplish political and economic ends, namely to bring an end to the welfare state. He would recommend that the President cut taxes and then if the Congress did not cut spending, there would be a deficit and it would grow. Stockman explained it this way:

> "The success of the Reagan revolution depended upon the willingness of the politicians to turn against their own handiwork – the bloated budget of the American welfare state. Why would they do this? Because they had to! In the final analysis, I had made fiscal necessity the mother of political invention."[2]

It was not a long step from this to the Clinton Administration's determination to "end welfare as we know it." The myth of hard work and prosperity was embraced by enough Americans by the end of Reagan's second term that the country had overcome a recession in 1982 and a subsequent inflation, had become prosperous, and had built up a defense posture while the Soviet Union was visibly deteriorating, politically and economically. The President used the platform from previous presidential policies of negotiating with the USSR to encourage the political collapse of that country.

Reagan could inspire people with his words, and perhaps his acting career convinced him that for Presidents, words were more important than actions. When the hostages arrived home from Iran the week after his inauguration, he invited them to the Rose Garden. There he said to them, "Thank you for reminding us who we are." In a few words he encapsulated the message he wanted to convey to Americans: in their captivity, the hostages showed us that with courage and determination we can overcome anything.

The President had his problems, though, as all Presidents do. There was persistent trouble in the Middle East. In Lebanon the American Marine barracks in Beirut were bombed killing 261 Marines. They were there as peacekeepers.[3]

Reagan loved America, thought it was the hope of the world, the "last best hope of man..." He was a convinced anti-communist. He had dealt with communists in the movie industry, or thought he had, and was persuaded by the investigations that went on in Washington during the 1940s and 1950s that communism was a world-wide movement that recent history had shown could undermine a country's government through infiltration. The Alger Hiss case illustrated the problem. Many Americans also thought that we were threatened by communism and used their votes accordingly.

Foreign Policy

Reagan was the beneficiary of the work of previous Presidents going all the way back to Truman. Harry Truman dealt with "Uncle

Joe" Stalin himself, and the two had a short time of peace until the "iron curtain" Churchill spoke of rang down the length of Europe. Other Presidents and their Soviet counterparts were Eisenhower and Kennedy with Kruschev, Nixon with Brezhnev, Johnson with Kosygin (1967 in Glassboro) and Carter with Brezhnev. The Presidents' policies generally followed a line of threatening military action, but not using it unless and until some action by the Soviet Union or China, or governments seen as surrogates of those two, became a threat to the United States. Such threats were conceived as Soviet expansionism when Mr. X (George Kennan) recommended the containment policy. Later, such threats were seen as imminent military threats to this country, as in the Cuban missile crisis. The war in Vietnam was so conceived as was the North Korean invasion of the South decades earlier. The Berlin Wall was seen as a threat to Western economic hegemony in that city, where the Soviets controlled only one of its four sectors, while Britain, France and the United States controlled the other three in the post-war period. The ability of the Soviets to put their Sputnik in space was a potential threat and brought forth a flurry of activity by the United States to put its first satellites into space. That culminated in the moon landings. Each superpower built up its military strength as a threat to the other.

From their perspective, the Soviets perceived threats to their safety and interests too. These had primarily to do with the development of weapons by the United States. Especially threatening to the U.S.S.R. were the intercontinental ballistic missiles, and the possible use of nuclear weapons. Additionally, Ronald Reagan's proposed defense shield to protect his country from incoming missiles, the "Star Wars" concept, was seen as a threat by the Russians.

The perception of the American people that it was Reagan who resolved the issues between the Soviet Union and the United States was cultivated by the President, but the diligent and frustrating work of his several predecessors prepared the ground for that, as this brief history has shown. Reagan did, however, continue the belligerent posture toward the Soviet leaders who held office during his term, Andropov, Chernenko, and Gorbachev. In 1985, the President invited Gorbachev to meet with him, and a summit meeting was set for mid-November.[4] Reagan knew that the Soviet Union was in trouble, economically and politically. There was pressure from the society at large to resolve issues with the United States; the Russian public feared the bellicose-appearing Reagan, as did many Europeans. The Russian economy was stagnating and continued heavy expenditures for weapons to keep up with the United States appeared to be a losing proposition. So Gorbachev was glad to meet with the President, and over the next two years they were able to pave the way for peaceful relations which came to fruition in the Administration of George H.W. Bush. At Geneva in 1985, however, Reagan and Gorbachev argued back and forth about how to proceed with arms reductions. What should the respective arms negotiators accomplish? The Strategic Defense Initiative (SDI) being pursued by the Americans was what Gorbachev could not countenance. What the two did agree to was to meet again, next time at the invitation of Reagan to be held in the United States. They met at Reykjavik in October of 1986, and again in December, 1987 in Washington, then in Moscow in May, 1988 as Reagan's term was nearing its end, and finally in 1988 when Gorbachev addressed the United Nations. There he told the world,

> Today I can report to you that the Soviet Union has taken a decision to reduce its armed forces. Within the next two years their numerical strength will be reduced by 500,000 men. The number of conventional armaments will also be substantially reduced. This will be done unilaterally. By agreement with our Warsaw Treaty allies, we have decided to withdraw by 1991 six tank divisions from the German Democratic Republic, Czechoslovakia and Hungary, and to disband them . . [5].

He went on to announce other decreases, all done without negotiation with the United States or European powers. Americans were amazed at this change in direction in the Soviet Union. It was accompanied by a change in the Soviet Central Committee membership and the structure of that Committee and the Party running the government. These changes took place after the American election and a new President, George H. W. Bush, would take the oath of office in a month.

This last encounter was at a luncheon on Governor's Island in New York after Gorbachev's speech to the UN. Throughout these meetings, and those held at other times with Secretary of State George Shultz meeting with Gorbachev and other Soviet leaders, the position of the United States was that we will not reduce our armaments until the Soviets state a willingness to do the same. Both governments wanted to reduce the high cost of armaments and relieve the world of the threats of nuclear or conventional war. The Soviets had a greater need than the Americans to dramatically reduce the costs of armaments. So in a sense, they were the first to blink.[6] Reagan had held to a firm position throughout the summit meetings that the Soviets must become serious about reducing tensions: "Tear down this wall," show good faith by removing troops and weapons from Eastern Europe. Since these issues were the ones that had governed the minds and decisions of nations since the end of World War II, President Reagan deserved credit for staring down the Soviets and gaining peace between the superpowers. But the same posture had been held by his predecessors going back to Harry Truman, so all of those Presidents can be credited with the victory of peace and no war with the Soviet Union

President Reagan in Berlin, "no war with the Soviet Union"
Source: Ronald Reagan Presidential Library. Date: 12 June 1987
Author: White House Photographic Office

Reagan had other foreign policy concerns to deal with: the Middle East, principally with the Israelis and Palestinians, but also with Syria and about the weak Lebanon. American Marines had been sent to Beirut to help protect the country from threats by the Israelis or the Syrians. Reagan remembered the disaster of the bombing of the American Marine barracks where 261 Marines were killed. The American embassy in Beirut had also been bombed at that time. It was believed that these actions were carried out by Islamic terrorists, but possibly by Syrians.

Reagan also had several rounds with terrorists who were hijacking airliners and ships in the Middle East. On one ship, an American passenger, Leon Klinghoffer, suffered a tragic death after being thrown overboard in his wheelchair. Because the Americans were usually on the receiving end of these actions, they made bad publicity in the United States, especially since the government was focused on rescuing hostages but not retaliating on the perpetrators. Much of that was the result of the inability to fix responsibility. In the case of one hijacked airliner, however, on Reagan's order American planes surrounded the plane and forced it to land in Sicily.[7]

Finally, Reagan was concerned about Central American countries that he thought were susceptible to a communist takeover as Cuba had been. He was most concerned about Nicaragua and El Salvador. The Sandinista government of Nicaragua was Marxist and El Salvador was ruled by a business-military government which was opposed by a left-wing group of guerrilla fighters who were trying to overthrow it. President Reagan believed that the situation in both countries threatened the security of the United States. The government of Nicaragua was supporting the insurgents in El Salvador, and as Reagan saw it, both countries could become satellites of the Soviet Union. He was determined to not "lose" Central America to the communists. So he pressed Congress to provide funds for assistance to El Salvador, while the CIA was doing what it could to destabilize the government in Nicaragua, by recruiting and training the "contras." An election in El Salvador, was won by Jose Napoleon Duarte, a Christian Democrat who was preferred by the Reagan Administration. Congress approved the aid package Reagan sought for El Salvador. However, Congress was not willing to continue to fund the "contra" war in Nicaragua. The President decided to look for outside help, and had Bud McFarlane, his director of the National Security Council, secretly approach the Saudis for money, about a million dollars a month, in exchange for two Air Force tankers with crews and 400 Stinger ground-to-air missiles and 200 launchers.[8]

Reagan's handling of aid to the contras became circuitous when his funding requests to Congress were turned down. The result was the continuing sale of weapons to Iran, using part of the proceeds to bolster the contras in Nicaragua. It also involved arms for the hostages in Beirut. This became a scandal, as Congress began investigating. A Marine Lt. Colonel, Oliver North, was carrying Reagan's baggage, but the several investigations and news stories finally concluded that yes, North had acted under orders and the President's Director of the National Security Council Admiral John Poindexter. By the time all the revelations had been made, North, Poindexter, George Shultz, and Bud McFarlane were charged with criminal acts in the sale of arms to Iran for money to be used to support the contras. It was criminal as contrary to the Constitution to sell and buy from a foreign country without Congressional approval of the use of funds and weapons. But it involved much more by the time it was all over: the officials in the White House lied to each other, lied to investigators, and on and on.[9]

McFarlane had testified truthfully to the Tower Commission set up to investigate independently. He thought the President would back him up if he were ever asked about the matter. McFarlane had the shock of his life when Reagan gave his State of the Union message in 1987, and "comfortably slipped past responsibility and talked only about putting this unpleasantness behind him. McFarlane felt abandoned. He thought he was the only one willing to talk and willing to tell the truth. He was alone."[10] A short time later, McFarlane tried to commit suicide, but was found by his wife, hospitalized, and regained consciousness a day later. This event, coupled with CIA Director Casey's collapse two months before with a brain tumor, kept the news media active.[11] Reagan's response to questions about the investigations and the work of his subordinates was essentially, "no one told me." There were resignations and removals, and a new set of top staff and cabinet members joined the Administration.

Whether it was good policy to send weapons to Iran in exchange for hostages in Beirut and some money given to the contras in Nicaragua remains a question for policy analysts. It was illegal, and clearly contrary to the intent of Congress. It was a matter of the

President defying the legislative body because he wanted to pursue his own policy. He thought he knew better.

More on the Economy

In spite of the Iran-contra scandal, Reagan and his Chairman of the Federal Reserve Board could take credit for a remarkable turnaround of the economy. Paul Volcker had been appointed by President Carter in 1979. The Chairman and his Board exercised their power to regulate the supply of money in the economy and that had the desired effect of significantly reducing inflation. It had dropped to 5% by 1983, and Reagan reappointed Volcker. The austerity that people felt from the Volcker treatment essentially made it harder to get credit as the Fed used its powers to set the prime rate of interest in order to rein in inflation. This plan paid off in several years as individual income taxes came down, the top rate down from 70% to 33 %. Interest rates came down too, and unemployment dropped to 6.1%. As one of Reagan's biographers pointed out,

> But even though each year after 1981 the Congress and the President had conspired to raise taxes and fees by more than $80 billion a year -- usually calling it "tax reform" or "closing loopholes" – economic expansion was being financed not by greater savings and new investment but by budget deficits averaging $172 billion a year, doubling the national debt in just six years.[12]

The United States had become a debtor nation. There were more rich people, and they became richer, while the poor became poorer. By 1987, twenty-five percent more American children were living in poverty than did in 1980. As a biographer wrote, "Politically, Reagan repealed Lyndon Johnson's 'Great Society' – and chipped away, too, at the New Deal of Franklin D. Roosevelt." [13]

The Iran-contra hearings were in recess as Congress took two weeks off in June, 1987. The Joint House-Senate Committee investigating the Iran-contra matter announced that the hearings would resume in July with Colonel North and Admiral Poindexter. In the interim, President Reagan went to Berlin on the occasion of the 750th birthday of the city. It was on this trip that he made his famous challenge to the Soviet leader, Gorbachev: "Mr. Gorbachev, tear down this wall!" It was memorable politics, a diversion for the American public and Reagan's own statement to the Soviet leader about freedom.

THE ECONOMY IN 2000

Over the Twentieth Century, the changes in the economy were as dramatic as those in the country itself. In Theodore Roosevelt's America the nation was emerging from a rural society into an industrializing one, a society that had large numbers of people at the lower end of the income scale and a small number at the top. This was the Gilded Age, when the "robber barons" and the "plutocrats" dominated the manufacturing jobs and the markets traded their products. It was the period in which Presidents like T.R. tried to manage the economy by preventing the tendency toward monopoly of the big businesses like steel, the railroads, and the oil industry. He believed that competition would keep business practices fair. The Age was Gilded, though, by the extremes of wealth that the successful businessmen were able to achieve. Paul Krugman calls this the Long Gilded Age; it lasted from 1870s to the 1930s when, to deal with the Great Depression, government under the leadership of Franklin Roosevelt sponsored laws to stimulate and regulate the economy.

Going beyond anti-monopolistic measures, the New Deal created a number of agencies to regulate the buying and selling of stocks in the stock exchanges. The Securities and Exchange Commission was created to protect investors, assure fairness in securities trading, publish information about the markets, and oversee the exchanges. There were laws to permit laborers to unionize and bargain collectively with management to obtain decent wages, shorter hours, and better working conditions. A minimum wage law was passed by the Congress as was unemployment insurance. Support prices for agricultural products protected farmers. There were laws that created programs to provide a social safety net: old age assistance until the Social Security program could take hold, aid to the permanently and totally disabled, aid to the blind, and aid to families with dependent children. In 1937, the nation's first public housing act was passed, a program urged by some of the country's big cities, for example, New York and Chicago. The Federal Trade Commission was created to protect consumers from false advertising and illegal business practices. A Federal Power Commission was created to assure by regulation the safe manufacture and distribution of power across the country, including electric power and natural gas. The Federal Reserve Board of Governors of the Federal Reserve Bank of the United States, created in 1914, continued its job of setting interest rates that banks use to loan to each other.

In addition to these regulatory agencies to support the free enterprise system and prevent fraud and abuse, the New Deal undertook to infuse large amounts of money into the economy via such programs as the Tennessee Valley Authority and the Works Progress Administration. Various public works were begun in the New Deal years, such as construction of dams to generate electric power. The vast infusion of government money to fight the Second World War, however, was the program that moved the country out of the Depression. There came to be an equalizing effect from the New Deal's programs that Krugman calls the Great Compression. It lasted from about 1930 to about 1980.

There were three periods in the post-war economy: the post-war boom, from 1947 to 1973, then, from 1973 to 1980 there was what Krugman calls the time of troubles, with crises in obtaining enough oil to run American industry and American cars. The third period saw "reasonable growth" of the economy but with rising inequality of incomes. This period from 1980 to 2007 Krugman names the New

Gilded Age. So if we can picture this history of income inequality in America for the Long Gilded Age we would see two horizontal lines, the upper one rising and the lower one declining so that there was a growing gap between them. With the Depression and the Second World War, the lines moved closer to parallel and the space between them became smaller. This was a time of the growth of a substantial middle class, and inequalities of income were not so large. Krugman calls this the Great Compression. During this time, taxes were raised to pay for the war and for the post-war projects that aided the recovery from three-and-one-half years of deterioration of the nation's infrastructure caused by lack of funds and attention. Later in the 1960s, Lyndon Johnson's Great Society programs also contributed substantially to the improving condition of the lower income groups, programs such as Medicare, Model Cities urban programs, the Education Act of 1967, and the Fair Housing Act of 1968. The Civil Rights Act and the Voting Rights Act contributed to the ability of minority groups to train for and get good jobs.

There was a system that Krugman calls "pattern wages" that came out of labor-management agreements in the 1950s and 1960s. This described a condition where the wage settlements of the large industrial unions acted as a restraint on the incomes of both management and stockholders. The support by the federal government of the bargaining positions of labor supported this pattern. In those years there was an agreement between the auto industry and labor unions called the "Treaty of Detroit" wherein labor received health and retirement benefits from industry in return for no strikes or demands from the unions.

Taxes were high for the upper income groups and corporations into the 1970s, the highest tax bracket being 70%. The New Gilded Age has seen a lowering of those taxes for the highest income groups, and at the same time there was pressure to reduce or remove regulations from certain industries. There came to be resentment toward entitlement programs which had been designed for poor people who could not make it on their own. The ones grouped under the term "welfare" rankled with the middle class as well as with the wealthy. Taxes came down, so that the highest bracket by the end of the 1990s was set at 35%.

Krugman makes the case that institutions and norms rather than technology or globalization are the main sources of inequality in the United States today. The collapse of the trade union movement is an example of an institutional change. This movement collapsed in part because of the practice of "union busting" used by some businesses. Krugman cites examples: during the late 1970s and early 1980s, at least one of every 20 workers was fired for voting for a union.[1] Attitudes toward unions were significantly different in European countries in the same period, although their economies had undergone a similar Great Compression in the middle of the Century.

The norms in the United States reversed the New Deal and Great Society programs and philosophy in that period, but the same did not happen in Europe where bloated incomes of a business class are disapproved of and labor generally receives entitlements. More recently, with the financial collapse in 2008, there was a loss of public tolerance for the CEOs of America's great corporations with their huge salaries and bonuses and, when departing, their golden parachutes.

Deregulation is the other important feature of the changes that have occurred to create a New Gilded Age in the United States. Both Republican and Democratic Presidents proposed and carried out some aspect of deregulation in the belief that such steps would bring down prices for which there was public demand. In the 1970s, for example, air fares were high and the Carter Administration brought them down through deregulation. This policy helped the consumer but did not reduce inflation as Carter had hoped it would.

These were the early years of deregulation; it was expected by politicians and economists alike that with lower prices for the consumer and a reduced burden of regulations, a variety of private and public services would encourage a more prosperous economy.

Krugman's major point was that because of income inequality over the last decades of the Twentieth Century, the middle class shrank in number and in economic weight. Krugman believes that extremes of wealth and poverty in a society are harmful for a democratic system, and that the policies of the government that are most harmful are those that deregulate important economic functions in the society. Deregulation allows the large corporations to acquire ever more of the public wealth. He writes,

> The fact is that vast income inequality inevitably brings vast social inequality in its train. And this social inequality isn't just a matter of envy and insults. It has real, negative consequences for the way people live in this country....It matters a great deal that millions of middle-class families buy houses they can't really afford, taking on more mortgage debt than they can safely handle, because they're desperate to send their children to a good school – and intensifying inequality means that the desirable school districts are growing fewer in number, and more expensive to live in.[2]

The idea of equality of opportunity is largely fictitious, he says, and the reasons are several. One is the lack of universal health care. Many children from low-income families are not insured and if they have health problems, they cannot fare very well as they grow up. They often have poor nutrition and this has long-term effects. Education in the United States is uneven and this affects the chances for children to get a higher education as they get older. Not only does the wealth of a small number of people give them inordinate influence with government through their political contributions, but also in society at large. Krugman says, "More broadly still, high levels of inequality strain the bonds that hold us together as a society." He notes the fact that people are less likely to trust each other, not to mention trust government, than was the case 40 years ago.[3] We know what government can do to encourage greater equality among income groups: adopt a universal health care plan, restore regulations where necessary to restrain those who know how to acquire vast sums of money, and improve education chances for our children.

GEORGE HERBERT WALKER BUSH
1989-1993

The first President George Bush had a reputation as a thoroughly decent man. Raised in Greenwich, Connecticut, in a culture of restraint and propriety he was taught by his mother that he should never brag about himself, and taught by his father, Senator Prescott Bush, what service to the country meant. The Bush children were taught about duty to others, to family and to country. There is a story that when the children would go out to see a friend or go to another's house, Dorothy Bush would say to them "Have a nice time, your Excellency." They were taught that they were ambassadors from their family to the other family, and should behave accordingly. Thinking of the good of others was important, and representing their family well was also important. There was a Puritan streak in this Eastern Republican ethos; display of self and possessions was frowned upon. Understatement and modesty were the proper attitudes. Hard work and diligence were expected of the men; women were taught to be conspicuous by being inconspicuous. By the example of the older women, however, the younger ones learned early that it was their duty to run the household and raise the children.

Official portrait of George H.W. Bush, circa 1989.
Courtesy Wikimedia Commons
Author: N/A, likely POTUS

One of the behaviors passed down through the Bush family was that the young men were expected to decide on their calling early and should challenge their fathers in so doing, but always in respectful ways. When George was approaching the age when he could join the military service, the advent of war after the attack on Pearl Harbor was the catalyst for his decision to tell his father that he was not going to Yale, he was going to join the Navy.[1] Prescott had done that in his turn; as America entered the First World War, he volunteered for the Yale Battalion. George wanted to fly airplanes. In fact, he distinguished himself; flying some 116 bombing runs. He was shot down over the Pacific, but he carried out the bombing mission assigned to him from his wounded plane. Then he parachuted from the plane, landing in the ocean. He was spotted on his life raft by an American submarine, and he was rescued. He was decorated for his heroism. The young Bush could have stayed in Connecticut after he finished Yale, and might well have moved into politics there. But he didn't want to do that, he wanted to launch out on his own. With the help of his father's connections in Texas, he took his young wife Barbara and his son George to Texas where he went into the oil business.[2]

Poppy Bush, a family name given by his uncles, served two terms as a Congressman from his Houston district. Later, he was appointed Director of the CIA, and President Ford appointed him to the American liaison office in China before formal diplomatic relations were established. He had served in the Nixon Administration as Ambassador to the United Nations and later as Chairman of the Republican National Committee.[3] During the latter service, which included the Watergate hearings, he was shocked by the slowly emerging truth about the burglary. He was especially shocked by Nixon's lies and the lies told by the people surrounding him. In a letter he wrote to his four sons on July 23. 1974, he described his feelings. He was torn, was appalled by the "abysmal amorality" of the government's actions. He said, nevertheless, that he thought Nixon had done excellent work in bringing the Vietnam War to an end, and in other foreign policy initiatives. Moreover, he had been personally kind to Bush. However, Bush could not countenance the fact that the President had lied outrageously about his role in Watergate, that in fact he had participated in the decisions and later tried to cover up the crime.[4]

George Bush ran for President in 1980, but Ronald Reagan won the nomination. Reagan then asked Bush if he would run with him for Vice-President and Bush agreed. In all the campaigning that year and his eight years of service as Vice-President, Bush kept himself loyal to Reagan, and to some degree effaced himself and his own policy beliefs. This tendency to avoid self-advancement in deference to teamwork and loyalty to the leader marked Bush's years as Vice-President. People, especially the press, did not understand that behavior and did not know where it came from so they called it weakness, the "wimp factor." This was used in the election campaign of 1988.[5]

Foreign Policy

The Middle East continued to be on every President's agenda during the 1980s and 1990s. Ronald Reagan and King Fahd of Saudi Arabia communicated privately but also held a summit meeting and state dinner in 1985.[6] It will be remembered that Reagan had tapped King Fahd for money in the effort to support the contras in Nicaragua.

The Bush family also had connections with the monarchy of Saudi Arabia, a relationship that had originated in the Bin Laden land development business but became important in the oil business. The patriarch, Mohammed Bin Laden, was an architect and building contractor, a self-made man who came to Saudi Arabia from Yemen and developed his construction business.

By the 1980s, the Bin Laden family was heavily invested in the United States "in shopping centers, apartment complexes, condominiums, luxury estates. . . corporate stocks, an airport and much else. They attended American universities, maintained friendships and business partnerships with Americans, and sought American passports for their children. They financed Hollywood movies, traded thoroughbred horses with country singer Kenny Rogers, and negotiated real estate deals with Donald Trump. They regarded George H.W. Bush, Jimmy Carter, and Prince Charles as friends of their family."[7]

Now, with the Bush presidency the Saudis had an interest in what America would do in the aftermath of the Iran-Iraq War. The Saudis had supported the Iraqis against Iran which the desert kingdom perceived as threatening to its interests, particularly its religion. Iran was and is a Shi'a Muslim country; Saudi Arabia is Sunni Muslim as was the regime of Saddam Hussein in Iraq. Religious differences in the politics of the Middle East have always been important. Nevertheless, the Saudis felt threatened by Saddam as did other Middle Eastern countries. When Saddam's army marched into Kuwait, there was a widespread fear that he would move further and threaten the free access to oil in both Kuwait and Saudi Arabia and other countries. Access can be controlled by closing the Strait of Hormuz through which ships passed in and out of the oil rich region.

It is very upsetting for any President to send American young men into battle, and it was no less so for George Bush. In the period between the end of World War II and Vietnam, the National Conference of Catholic Bishops published its statement concerning the reasons that could justify a nation in going to war.[8] This statement was highly respected in the United States. An unprovoked attack could justify a military response, but this case was not directly an attack on the United States. It was, however, a threat to a vital resource, oil, which this country and a significant number of other countries relied on to support their economies. A coalition of concerned nations needing to protect their petroleum resources could, in the minds of many, justify military action. Another question about going to war concerned its degree of battle intensity, the kind of weapons used and the clear statement of objectives. Weapons used and the military tactics should be proportional to the objectives. To drive Saddam out of Kuwait was the objective. The reason it was essential was to prevent Iraq from moving on to Saudi Arabia and its oil resources after it had conquered Kuwait and installed a puppet government there.

Bush and other Western leaders were seriously concerned with this threat and the President worked the telephones to build a coalition of nations who would be willing to send troops to drive the Iraqi troops back out of Kuwait. An offer was made to King Fahd of Saudi Arabia to send American troops to that country, stationing them there to be ready for whatever military action was required. Meanwhile, the President first began his action against Saddam with "Desert Shield" in August which became "Desert Storm" in January when it was clear military action was required. Joining the United States forces of almost one-half million troops, were 118,000 troops from allied nations. The decision was made by the American command and by the President that they should not undertake a drive to Baghdad but conclude military action when the Iraqi army was clearly beaten and out of Kuwait. The land war lasted 100 hours. Television viewers could see the path of destruction waged by Saddam himself when he had fires set wherever oil wells could be found in Kuwait. It appeared that the entire route of retreat by the Iraqi army was on fire.

George Bush is not a Catholic, but he did need to take into account the Catholic Bishops' statement and the considered opinion of responsible people, like Cardinal Law and Episcopal Bishop Browning from Bush's own church.[9] It is in this context that he concluded, along with his military advisers, that the coalition force should not pursue the Iraqi army all the way to Baghdad. The President was widely praised for his firm action and his restraint in the end. The objective, to drive Saddam out of Kuwait, was achieved.

The victory in Iraq plus several decisions by the United Nations began a program of sanctions to prevent Saddam from developing nuclear, biological and chemical weapons. As so often happens when international institutions and governments use sanctions to bring an international offender to heel, these actions had most of their effect on the people of Iraq. It is always hoped that the public will rise up and resist or get rid of a bad ruler like Saddam because he is the one depriving the people of what they need. But they usually don't rise up. They are afraid. And they suffer deprivations. The decisions of the UN continued to prevail into the new century.

President Bush was the beneficiary of the years of negotiation with the Soviet Union by his predecessors in the office. In December, 1989, the Berlin Wall was torn down by Germans who wanted a reunited country, separated for so long into East Germany and West Germany. Pieces of the Wall were sold around the world as gifts. There had been successes and delays and, for many years, a kind of stasis in U.S.-Russian relationships. But the tearing down of the Wall became a kind of catalyst for change in the Communist empire. In 1991, the Soviet Union collapsed politically and its many regional structures broke away from Moscow and became independent republics. Eastern European countries gained their freedom and in Russia, the government was reorganized with new leadership in office, notably Mikhail Gorbachev and then Boris Yeltsin. Both men were grateful to President Bush for the support he gave them when a "coup" by other elements in the Soviet Union was threatening. The effect on the peoples of Western countries was relief and joy when the old Soviet Union was gone and Russia could look forward to a new day.

Events in the Western Hemisphere centered on the drug trade. President Bush was concerned as was his predecessor with the threat of communist governments in Central America and the drug trade from that region into the United States. In Panama, the President ordered troops to land in Panama and seize General Manuel Noriega who was a threat to the Panama Canal, so vital to trade between East and West. He was also involved in the drug trade and was brought to the United States to be tried on that count.

The Economy

President Bush was a natural leader in world affairs, and his greatest successes came in his foreign policy leadership. He had domestic problems with the economy, however, with a recession and unemployment reaching unacceptable levels. In the Fall of 1990 he worked with Congress to bring a resolution to these problems, specifically the budget. Unhappily, this meant a tax increase along with some spending cuts. Bush was roundly criticized for the tax increase because in his 1988 election campaign he had pledged no new taxes. But it was salutary for the country, as he explained in a later note,

> Through a combination of tax increases and spending cuts, (the bill) slashed the accumulated deficit by $500 billion over five years. We also set strict limits on discretionary spending. I will confess to feeling a little vindicated in 1998 when the federal budget deficit was finally erased and a number of economists, journalists, and government officials cited 'Bush's 1990 budget compromise' as the beginning of the end of our deficit problem.[10]

So many achievements and successes for an American Administration might have predicted a second term for President Bush, but it was not to happen. Presidential historian Michael Beschloss wrote,

> Bush emerged from the Gulf War in March 1991 with a public approval rating of 91 percent, but with the recession in earnest some political advisers proposed that he wage an 'Operation Domestic Storm' to strengthen the economy and address other domestic problems ignored during Bush's first two years. The President refused. He saw his Gulf victory, the approaching end of the Cold War and his commanding popularity as a vindication of his decision to concentrate on world affairs. Calling attention to the weak economy would merely damage public confidence and prolong the recession. And who could unhorse a President so clearly indispensable in foreign policy? Rather than respond to increasing signs of public discomfort, he looked the other way.[11]

WILLIAM JEFFERSON CLINTON
1993-2001

Official White House photo of President Bill Clinton
Source: http://www.dodmedia.osd.mil/DVIC
Author: Bob McNeely, The White House

Bill Clinton was the classic "baby boomer." He grew up in a generation that got involved in all kinds of political and social issues. They engaged in demonstrations for various causes, particularly those concerned about seeking equity and justice at home and protesting war abroad. He partook of the youth culture of the time: sampling drugs and marijuana (which he did not inhale) and deafening themselves with hard rock music. They brought into the real world the sexual revolution. Now, it was all right to talk about sex and engage in it.

More important, however, was Clinton's love of politics and his desire to do something for his country that would benefit it far more than military service in Vietnam could do, especially since he did not approve of the war. He found out early that his interest would be in the domestic economy with which governments since Nixon had struggled. Either inflation had to be tamed or the budget deficit which David Stockman thought he had conquered had to be reduced. Something had to be done about domestic expenditures by government, especially on those problem budget items like "welfare" or other "entitlements." Ultimately, new ways had to be found to make America prosperous. He thought that one way would be to expand "free trade." His education and his quick mind understood what was happening in the world: globalization. From this platform of comprehension, Clinton could think of running for President.

Because Bill Clinton likes people and exudes charm, many influential people helped him. He had developed good friendships and supporters in Arkansas where he grew up, such as Senator William Fulbright, and Wilbur Mills, the Chairman of the House Ways and Means Committee. He applied to Georgetown University's School of Foreign Service and was accepted. After college, Clinton went to work for Senator Fulbright as a member of his staff. The Senator, himself a former Rhodes Scholar, wrote a letter of recommendation for Bill; he was selected and prepared to go to Oxford University.[1]

His early life with his family in Hope, Arkansas would not have predicted this future for the boy. His stepfather was a car dealer and an alcoholic. He was abusive to his wife. Young Bill Clinton is remembered for having stood up to the man even as he loved him. He also took his last name for his own, because his real father, William Blythe, had been killed in a car accident before the boy was old enough to know him. A difficult childhood for Bill Clinton, but he overcame it with his intelligence, his optimism and his likeability.

Having worked for Senator Fulbright, Clinton enrolled in the ROTC along with his enrollment in the University of Arkansas law school. Between his two years at Oxford, he received his draft letter and realized that he might not be able to finish his second year there. When he returned to Arkansas in the summer of 1969, he applied for and obtained a deferment for his remaining year at Oxford. He promised to resume his ROTC status after the final year at Oxford, expecting to attend the University of Arkansas Law School. However, during that year, the Nixon Administration redesigned the draft using a lottery system, so that a man's draft number was left to chance. When Clinton came back the following summer, his military service status had changed, and ultimately he was not called up before the war's end.

The change gave him the opportunity to apply to Yale Law School; he was accepted. There he met Hillary Rodham whom he later married. He spent two years studying the law, taking time as necessary to work on the election campaign of a candidate for the U.S. Senate, Joe Duffey of Connecticut. Two years later, he worked on the McGovern for President Campaign. His taste for politics grew the more he worked on campaigns. When he moved back to Arkansas, he again got involved in politics, building a network and helping other candidates in their election campaigns. Then he decided to run for Governor of the State. He won the office and in his two terms was able to help improve the economy of the

State. So in due course, Clinton announced he was a candidate for President.

The Clinton-Gore campaign of 1992 had verve. They won their nominations for President and Vice-President at the Democratic National Convention and then, with their wives Hillary and Tipper, they boarded their campaign bus for a trip through the Midwest. Their youthful enthusiasm was contagious. In the November election, however, Ross Perot entered the lists as a third party candidate, or an independent, whichever way he wanted to classify himself. This prevented any of the three candidates, Bush, Clinton, and Perot, from winning 50% of the electoral vote, or the popular vote. Nevertheless, Clinton won the election with 43% of the electoral vote.[2]

The Economy

If Clinton's predecessor in the White House, George H.W. Bush, had wanted to be a foreign policy President, Bill Clinton wanted to be a domestic policy President. From his experience in State politics, and as Governor of Arkansas he had policy ideas, particularly about the economy. At the national level, he wanted to reduce the annual deficit, or better yet, end it and balance the budget. One of the vehicles that he would use to this end was foreign trade. He recognized the significance of globalization and thought trade was central to economic progress for the United States.

The debt service for the national debt, and the annual deficit, were fiscal restraints sufficient finally to require significant cutbacks in government spending. There were some people in the country who had protested for years that welfare was bad policy, that it encouraged dependency, and that dependents will avoid work in order to avoid being self-supporting. So when Clinton was ready to propose a new system that would help people but would also require them to work there was a public that agreed with him. It took some time to get other elements of the society, and especially the Congress to accept the idea. But finally, Clinton announced to the American people that the legislation he was proposing would mark the "end of welfare as we know it" in this country.

The largest part of the annual deficit and its growth was the continual sixty-year requirement for national defense during the Cold War and the Vietnam War. Presidents and Congresses had to handle first the security of the country, and this involved every year a huge expenditure for military hardware, services, people and related costs. But with the end of the Cold War, the government looked for ways to reduce these expenditures. In the eight years of the Clinton Administration, there was no major war, although there was a military involvement with NATO to bring peace to the warring ethnic groups in the former Yugoslavia. For the United States, this was primarily air support.

Several elements came together to help President Clinton propose a balanced budget as his second term approached its end. The "workfare" program had begun to take effect on the economy, reducing government expenditures for the former Aid to Families With Dependent Children, usually called welfare.[3] In addition, however, because it was peacetime, there could be reduced military expenses. Especially important, was the prosperity the country enjoyed in the '90s. That brought in more tax revenue at relatively constant tax levels. From the first budget of his Presidency, cutting the deficit was priority number one. The Administration reduced government expenditures each year during the '90s. The net effect was a budget surplus by the end of his term in 2000. As the country looked ahead to the new millennium, it seemed poised to reap the benefits of so many years of collective stress, and to enjoy prosperity.

In foreign policy issues, Clinton worked to reduce trade barriers for all nations, believing that all would benefit from freer trade. This policy had governed American policy in the Western Hemisphere for decades and was an important objective for Presidents of both political parties. The North American Free Trade Agreement was finally approved and went into effect in 1994, during Clinton's first term. Former Presidents were invited to the signing ceremony, emphasizing the bipartisan nature of the agreement.[4] This was important because in Congress the bill had traveled a rocky road. The AFL-CIO opposed it believing that it would cause a loss of jobs in this country. Environmentalists opposed it believing that anti-pollution standards in the United States would be compromised in the other two countries, Mexico and Canada. Clinton wanted some side deals to respond to both of those objections, and finally got them. There would be both labor and environmental standards that would be binding on Mexico.[5] About the agreement, Clinton said,

> I made that case that NAFTA would be good for the economies of the United States, Canada and Mexico, creating a giant market of nearly 400 million people; that it would strengthen U.S. leadership in our hemisphere and in the world; and that failure to pass it would make the loss of jobs to low-wage competition in Mexico more, not less, likely. Mexico's tariffs were two and a half times as high as ours, and even so, next to Canada, it was the largest purchaser of U,S, products. The mutual phaseout of tariffs had to be a net plus to us.[6]

The United States had agreed with Canada to a free trade relationship between the two countries in 1989, and they in turn broadened the agreement to include Mexico in the early 1990s. Political campaigns of later years launched attacks on NAFTA and a later Central American Free Trade Agreement because such agreements were responsible for job losses of many U.S. workers. However, the benefits of free trade were also evident. Writing of the effects of Clinton's policies for NAFTA and also for the Asia-Pacific Economic Community and the General Agreement on Tariffs and Trade, the foreign policy scholar, George C. Herring, said "The Clinton administration eventually presided over an enormous expansion of U.S. foreign trade, sparking one of the nation's longest periods of economic growth."[7] So there were tradeoffs resulting from NAFTA and related agreements.

As Thomas Friedman has explained in his book *The World is Flat*, all measures of the economies of countries around the world show that their relationships are changing rapidly and meaningfully. There is much more of a level playing field among the nations of the world; other nations were competing with the U.S. and this country would have to adapt to the flattening and adjust its policies to meet the new conditions.[8] President Clinton likely perceived some elements of the changes occurring during his eight years in office. He picked up the free trade program, NAFTA, of the Republicans and carried it through to approval by the Democrat controlled Senate. He also understood the aspiration of George H.W. Bush for the United States to play an active role in the development of a "new world order." The changing economies could be seen as part of the new world order.

Foreign Policy

Events in Europe, notably the ethnic war in the former Yugoslavia, made it clear that NATO, the American-European military alliance, continued to be needed. The United States became the leader in putting down that conflict, a bitter hostility and frequent warfare carried on by ethnic Albanian Muslims and Christian Serbs for many decades. But this role was not happily taken by the administration. General Colin Powell, a Vietnam veteran and Chairman of the Joint Chiefs of Staff, was opposed to taking any military action where there was not a direct threat to the United States or its most vital interests.[9] The President was not eager to engage in the slaughter that was going on, so from 1992 until 1995, there was action taken by NATO in Bosnia but the U.S. was not directly involved.

There were people in Congress and the Administration, particularly Madeleine Albright who was appointed Secretary of State, who said that the United States had to be involved to protect human rights and bring about a peace. Finally, with U.S. approval, NATO began an intensive bombing campaign on Bosnian Serb positions. Colin Powell having completed his term, resigned from his Chairmanship of the Joint Chiefs, and other voices in favor of military action by the U.S. prevailed. The NATO bombing produced a cease fire and American diplomat Richard Holbrooke met with the warring parties in Dayton, Ohio, where the Dayton Accords were agreed to.[10] The agreement stipulated that Bosnia would be divided into a Muslim-Croat region and a Serb region and a NATO military force would maintain the cease-fire. American troops were sent to take part in the peacekeeping force. This was blown up by Albanian Muslims whose region, Kosovo, was not part of the peaceful settlement. They declared their independence and created their own army in 1997 and attacked the Serbs who responded in kind. The Serb leader Milosevic was defeated after the United States used its huge B-2 bombers flown to Europe from Missouri. Milosevic eventually was arrested and taken to Brussels and charged with crimes against humanity. He was tried by the special International Tribunal for the former Yugoslavia, but he died before the court had made its decision.[11]

Clinton also sought to help resolve the Northern Ireland fighting that persisted as frequent small wars between Catholics and Protestants. Through cooperation with the British Prime Minister, and the latter's request for a mediator, Clinton sent former Senator George Mitchell. After a lengthy time of periodic negotiation, Mitchell and representatives of the Catholics and Protestants in Northern Ireland, came out with the "Good Friday agreement."[12] While it did not end the controversy immediately, that agreement became the basis for settlement which was a reality within a year.

Considering how long the two sides had fought each other, the settlement was cause for rejoicing.

In a final foreign policy effort, President Clinton tried to resolve the decades-long fighting between the Palestinians and Israelis over the sovereignty and uses of land formerly considered Palestinian, and the rights of people displaced by the creation of the State of Israel in 1948. While he succeeded in getting Yasser Arafat and Ehud Barak to come to Camp David in the summer of 2000 and talk their way through the issues, he was unable to get them to agree on such important issues as the status of Jerusalem and the governance of Gaza and the West Bank.[13]

Social Stresses

The social stresses that emerged during the Clinton Presidency continued to include racial issues, but in addition there were pressures for gay rights and pressures to put an end to illegal immigration from south of the border. The availability of handguns was a continuing problem for which local and state governments tried to exact penalties.

The Clinton Administration took action on urban crime. With the federal grants provided by the Crime Bill, some 100,000 new police officers were on the streets of American cities. The Crime Bill also provided that criminals convicted of certain crimes had three chances to correct their behavior; after the three strikes, you were out. That could bring on a long prison term. This law was still being observed in 2008 in a number of states, notably California.[14]

Clinton was disappointed with the failure of his Israeli-Palestinian initiative, and humiliated by the memory of his impeachment for unbecoming behavior as President in the Monica Lewinsky affair. He was acquitted of the charges but the matter would not go away, the media keeping it alive. Many people were saddened to see on television a talented former President struggling to assert his contributions to America as he left the inauguration ceremony. Indeed, those contributions were substantial, especially in the economic and foreign policy areas.

After his retirement from the Presidency, Bill Clinton looked forward to an active life, which included major humanitarian projects around the world. His Clinton Foundations, set up in 2002, are concerned with health security with special attention to HIV/AIDS, developing leadership and citizen service, racial and religious reconciliation, and education. He had a serious heart attack but fortunately he received prompt medical care and recovered from it, if slowly.

The former Presidents Clinton and Bush were appointed by the younger President Bush to respond for the United States to the humanitarian crisis in Indonesia after a devastating tsunami struck the islands in 2004. Clinton continued his work raising money for the Foundations and wrote a book entitled *Giving*, a fitting message for those who have suffered a spiritual crisis as he had. He continued to be active in Democratic Party politics when his wife Hillary Clinton ran for President in 2008.

GEORGE WALKER BUSH
2001-2009

It is very difficult, and in some ways improper, to summarize a current Presidency. The further away from real people and real events one can be, the better the historical analysis. It is important to do justice to a person who has held high office and to his work. It is even difficult to review the performance of Bill Clinton as President, though he is eight years out of office at this writing. Nevertheless, some perspective on the man and his leadership has been gained even after that short a period of time.

What makes it acceptable to review George Bush's two terms of office before the new President has taken the oath is the fact that the events of the second term have brought about a coda of sorts to the trends that mark what America has been and the direction it appears to be going at the end of 2008. The conservative view of what the economy needs in a democratic country, the uses to which the military services should be put, and the style of relationship this country should have with others will be changing, one hopes for the better. Clearly, with the election of an African-American President, the United States has progressed significantly in its understanding of race relations. In this review, though, it is important to remember that all Presidents have their mistakes and policy failures. They also have successes, and these must balance the poor performance in

190

some areas. That being acknowledged, we consider the Presidency of George W. Bush.

Many people interested in politics and the Presidency were shocked and dismayed by some of the early decisions of President Bush. His rejection of the Kyoto Treaty entered into by a number of nations in Europe and Asia to deal with world climate change, and his rejection of available stem cells for research by scientists who believed the use of the knowledge they would gain could heal patients with serious diseases or disabilities were just two examples. Under existing law, the cell lines could not be used for research at all. Bush limited the cell lines that would be available to scientists to those existing at that time. He believed that widespread use of stem cells would be a violation of the right to life which was present in the cells. As for the Kyoto Treaty, environmentally conscious Americans hoped that even if that treaty could not be salvaged, with its stiff requirements, the President's outright rejection of it was a bad omen for the future in dealing with greenhouse gases. Bush also stated his intention to abrogate the Anti-Ballistic Missile Treaty.[4] This raised hackles in Moscow.

> He talked tough when the Chinese shot down a U.S. military plane violating their airspace and held its crew hostage. He spoke ambiguously about whether he supported continuing the long-standing policy of 'strategic ambiguity' with respect to Taiwan. He repudiated the Kyoto Accords on global warming. He spurned Yassir Arafat and stood by Ariel Sharon in Israel. He broke off negotiations with North Korea.[1]

While these actions seemed to suggest that there was a coherent foreign policy being developed by George W. Bush, in fact they reflected more of a search than a plan. The biographer, Jacob Weisberg, writes that "The botched search for a doctrine to clarify world affairs and the president's progressive descent into messianism"[2] are the result of Bush's inability to come to terms with the world. It became harder for him to confront after the attack on the United

States on September 11, 2001. Weisberg in his study of Bush 43 tries to understand the son's relationship with his father, Bush 41. There he concludes that the younger Bush alternately tried to gain his father's favor and tried to undo what his father had done about various policies when he was President, particularly his foreign policy. The invasion of Iraq, avoided by his father as inconsistent with the mission of "Desert Storm," is the prime example. By 2007, the negotiations with North Korea were underway again.

It is necessary to recognize the role of Vice-President Cheney in the Iraq war, and this is hard to do because he tended to work behind the scenes. Cheney had been the Secretary of Defense under the elder Bush, so he had credible judgment about what should be done after 9/11. His background in the oil business provided support for Bush's conviction that the United States had to secure its future resources for oil in the Middle East, where it was plentiful, although predictably limited through depletion. The lack of a defined and specific mission for the invasion of Iraq in 2003 allowed Secretary Rumsfeld and the Defense Department to make some significant mistakes: conducting the war with too few troops, allowing bureaucratic hang-ups to prevent the armoring of vehicles and delaying adequate response systems to some unique weapons used by the enemy. The IED's, or improvised explosive devices, were homemade by insurgents who used several different kinds of explosive materials. These were placed on the roadside by the enemy and were usually well-concealed so that American troops driving by would set them off. There were even more destructive weapons developed, it is believed in Iran, to continually threaten the American presence in Iraq. It was hard to achieve any kind of success for several years. Military leaders pointed out that this was an "asymmetrical war, an irregular war, a counterinsurgency war"[3] but the United States conducted its military forces to fight a conventional war.

General Petraeus, who was put in charge of the Iraq campaign in 2007, introduced a different kind of approach to this war. As retired

General Keane said to Secretary Rumsfeld, "We would move into a neighborhood and occupy some empty buildings that are not being used...The soldiers would eat there, sleep there and patrol there."[4] They would talk to Iraqis. Talking to merchants, talking to citizens, trust builds up. The traditional kind of warfare had prevented the Americans from eliminating the insurgents and promoting stability in neighborhoods of Baghdad and elsewhere in Iraq, but the Petraeus system was found to be successful. Finally, Bush and the Defense Department under Secretary Gates decided to send 20,000 more troops in 2007, and this had the desired effect of bringing more stability to the country. In the end, more than that number of troops was sent.

General Petraeus was given the Central Command in 2008 and General Odierno was placed in charge of the Iraq war. Nevertheless, there continued to be a few bombings by insurgents into the Fall of 2008. While conditions improved in Iraq, and a negotiated agreement was reached by the U.S. leadership and the Iraqi government about a departure of American troops by the end of 2011, some Iraqis and Americans did not agree with that date, preferring it to be much sooner than that, and Barack Obama, the President-elect, expected to withdraw most troops at an earlier date. Part of the agreement included a pull-back by American troops from the cities in the summer of 2009.

There is considerable objection to the Bush policies of detaining prisoners from the wars in Afghanistan and Iraq because the treatment of those people was directly contrary to some provisions in the Geneva Accords concerning treatment of prisoners. The Administration's policy of allowing torture to extract information from detainees also violates the Constitution's Bill of Rights. These issues will have to be worked out in the coming years by the Obama government. Moreover, the use of warrantless wiretapping of the telephones of citizens to elicit information about possible illegal activity or espionage in this country is unnecessary. The law allows wiretapping and electronic eavesdropping when a court order or warrant is issued to the investigating agency. This is done so that the action can be consistent with the Fourth Amendment's prohibition of unwarranted searches and seizures. Fear of delay in such cases is not a relevant reason for an investigating agency to act quickly without a warrant because the law allows a grace period when an investigation is urgent. What is important is the check and balance process: a magistrate can review a proposed eavesdropping plan and approve the action of an investigating agency. The law affords the government the security of providing reinforcement for the investigative agencies.

The Bush Administration can take credit for preventing further terrorist attacks on the United States and that has been a significant achievement. Surveillance at airports and other ports of entry together with agreements with other nations about inspecting passengers traveling to the United States have much to do with that success.

President Bush puts his arms around firefighter Bob Beckwith while standing on a crushed fire engine in front of the World Trade Center debris Sept. 14, 2001.

source:
"www.nydailynews.com/ny

President Bush himself presented Congress with a bill to resolve the concern for illegal immigration, particularly across our southern border. The public outcry against the possibility that illegal immigrants might be allowed to stay in the country and even qualify for citizenship after paying a fine for their illegal entry caused members of Congress to stop consideration of the bill and drop it. In the coming years, Congress is likely to again consider legislation on this subject.

The President made other significant contributions to foreign aid policies such as providing money for HIV/AIDS programs in Africa. His domestic program for children's education called No Child Left Behind was also an effort to make measurable improvement in their learning. The thought and effort that went into getting funding for this program makes incomprehensible the President's veto of a bill to provide States with funds for health insurance for uninsured children via State programs.

The President also has done much to advance the employment of blacks, Hispanics, Asian Americans and others in top positions of the government, for example Colin Powell and Condoleeza Rice. Ultimately, jobs and a degree of status is what will advance the cause of minorities in the United States. In fact, in recent years the growth of various population groups in the country is such that the word "minority" is meaningless.

The accomplishments of the Bush Administration are not balanced, however, by the economic disaster of 2008. It has been caused in significant part by the President's conviction that the right diet for the American economy is lowering taxes, especially for the well-to-do, deregulation and minimal regulation of such activities as financial institutions and other businesses like Wall Street investment firms. An important part of this philosophy has been that "government is the problem." These views together with the annual deficit built by the cost of two wars plus the "bailout" of important investment houses in late 2008 present a daunting perspective on the future of the United States.

SEEING THINGS WHOLE
1901-2008

The Twentieth Century brought broad changes to the lives of most Americans, and some of these changes were instigated by Presidents. Theodore Roosevelt helped people see that it is the duty of government to assure fairness in the free competition that should govern the relationships between businesses. He was President in the heyday of the dominance of the captains of industry, sometimes called the "Robber Barons." He thought that government had a duty to secure that fairness through anti-trust enforcement, and he urged a more enlightened treatment of the laboring man by business. Woodrow Wilson taught people, especially those in government, that peace for ourselves depended on collective action and organization with other nations. Franklin Roosevelt changed the lives of all of us with the programs designed to protect all Americans in our old age, in unemployment situations, in our disabilities, in the dependence of children whose parents could not support them.

Our lives were also profoundly changed by science, by the phenomenal growth of technology in advancing business and industry, by the great advances in medicine, and by much better knowledge about personal health. And, yes, by improved education in spite of the fact that the American public education system has been criticized for causing a leveling and weakening of learning in our society.

The widening of the income gap between rich and poor cannot be considered a benefit for the average person. Moreover, the deterioration in the standards of behavior and of social discourse degrades the quality of human life. There has been a brutalizing of social intercourse during the Twentieth Century. American politics and society are devoted to acquiring money and the things money can buy. This social phenomenon colors the culture to emphasize personal possessions. How else to understand the absurd status symbol of the latest model automobile.

Perhaps the most important change in our understanding of our economic relationships with each other is the recognition that the old laissez-faire attitude in business is dead. It was up-dated by Milton Friedman in the middle of the Century with his plea for less and less government regulation in businesses. He said that the road to freedom is capitalism, and that capitalism, if unfettered, would serve the freedom of everyone. But the crash of 2008 confirms what many of our Presidents have known, that raw competition had to be tamed with anti-trust laws and other regulations to keep the economic system fair, that social Darwinism is gravely hostile to the well-being of large numbers of people, and that when people are in financial trouble they need help and sometimes only the government can provide that help. Yet our system also worked out our problem of increasing dependence of people on government handouts when they actually could work for themselves. The Clinton policy of "ending welfare as we know it" opened the way to emphasis on job training and workfare. All these changes in our economic relationships resolved the issues we began with in 1901. The economic policy that did us in by 2008 was the theory that the workings of the market would balance the system, that deregulation was the solution to much that was wrong and that government was the problem.

Of course, Presidents have played strong roles in developing policies for the economy, for foreign policy and the reasons for going to war, and in some few cases policies to improve the economic and social condition of racial minorities. These several issue areas do show change, but always in the context of protecting what were believed to be the essential characteristics of a democratic system. There are various definitions of democracy, of course, and the definitions usually contain some element of economic well-being. So let's look at the changes in economic policy during the Twentieth Century.

The Economy

We entered the Century with a patrician President who confronted the problems he saw in the economic relationships within the industrial leadership of the country and between industry and labor. Teddy Roosevelt used his considerable persuasive powers to bring Congress to the realization that competition among industries often led to monopoly when the losing industry in that competition was bought out by the winner or was taken over by it. He believed in competition as the bedrock of a democratic industrial system. But steps had to be taken to oversee this system and keep it balanced between the forces continually at work, such forces as the self-interest of those engaging in the free enterprise system. The market for goods and services would automatically reach a balance following the law of supply and demand. He thought that monopoly was the factor that would cause imbalances, monopoly and the excessive greed of businessmen like those who ran the oil industry and charged exorbitant rates for distributing oil through their pipelines in New England. TR's gift to American society was his insistence that the upper classes had a duty to work for the public interest, to seek social justice as he did.

In the relationships that industries had with their workers, Roosevelt saw injustice and thought ways had to be found to balance the needs of the working man with the needs of the industries where they worked. As appeared in his later advocacy of the Progressive movement, his platform insisted on social justice. Industries must be made safe and the people who worked in them needed maximum hours protection. Workers should be paid a decent wage. Children should not have to work to help keep the family financially solvent. Women should be given jobs that are not physically harmful, and the hours they work must be consistent with the requirements they had to meet at home. He thought that everyone engaged in work, whatever the industry, should be able to create a healthy family environment. This view was the beginning of the aspiration for home ownership and a share of the so-called "American dream." Many of the benefits urged by TR and the Progressives became a reality only twenty years later, but there were some improvements during the 'Teens and '20s in such areas as hours of work required.

Theodore Roosevelt saw who was preventing progress in the economic relationships between labor and industry. He saw the Supreme Court as "in the pocket of the industrialists." Moreover, members of Congress had lobbyists in their train, lobbyists who argued against legislation such as the Hepburn Act. Roosevelt's influence, however, was felt by the Congressmen as well, and the bill was finally passed. Presidents Wilson, Herbert Hoover and Franklin Roosevelt all undertook further regulation believing that it was essential to the economy and also to social justice, in which all three believed.

The Century ended with conservatives declaring that government is the problem, that government should stay out of the affairs of business. President Jimmy Carter's Democratic Administration in the 1970s began deregulating certain industries: first, the airline industry, then trucking, telecommunications, petroleum prices, energy, and finance. He did these things to give relief to the consumer who was paying for the regulation as well as for products and services. Carter hoped that these steps would reduce inflation and give a boost to employment. When he left office, there had been an increase of almost 8 million jobs in the country. Inflation, however, would not respond to treatment and interest rates remained high. There was a recession.

When Ronald Reagan took office in 1981, he was confronted with the threat of a strike by airline controllers whose work was essential to the American transportation industry. Reagan told the controllers that any who engaged in a strike would be fired, under the authority of the President. When they did, he did. This was a public service industry and the President was empowered to fire people who interfered with the orderly conduct of a public service. This event plus the deregulation of a number of industries by Jimmy Carter, a Democrat, in the previous Administration, was enough to prove the point of the deregulators that the prices the public paid for the regulated services were too high and that the public and the government would all save money if some regulations were removed.

Deregulation did not mean that the affected industries had no oversight by government at all. The policy was deregulation of the prices paid by the consumer through introducing competition in certain industries; thus airline fares came down as a result of allowing competitive pricing. Laws governing the fair practices of businesses remained intact, and the myriad other relationships businesses had with the public and with each other continued to be regulated. Once the program of deregulation took hold, however, the conservatives in the Republican Party ran with the bit in their teeth. Deregulation would take other forms. The conviction grew that government was indeed the problem.

By the end of the first decade of the Twenty-first Century, however, the government, the finance industry, and particularly the private citizen paid a huge price for that philosophy. A major financial crisis developed in 2008 when there was a slow-down in the housing industry and this quickly spun out into a loss of confidence market-wide. So lax had the oversight by the government become that agencies that were supposed to see to it that home buyers had adequate financial backing to buy a home failed to do so. Particularly egregious was the practice by lenders of offering adjustable rate mortgages to people who wanted to buy a home. These instruments failed in large numbers because the purchasers could not pay their mortgages when interest rates ballooned. Government had failed to oversee banks and other lenders in their practices and the private citizen had become too accustomed to "easy credit." The enticements inviting people to get a credit card were legion and very seductive.

The Twentieth Century ended with a President in office who had been a Rhodes Scholar and an adept politician. President Clinton accomplished what his predecessors tried to do, balance the budget and eliminate the deficit that had appeared in the Federal budget annually for years. One way this was achieved was through the elimination of one welfare program, aid to families with dependent children. Heads of households who wanted assistance had to work, and a program of "workfare" was begun. So when welfare as an entitlement was ended, the American belief in work to support one's self and one's family was restored. Other entitlement programs were perhaps on the chopping block in the future; certainly the financial crisis at the end of 2008 brought this to the minds of many people.

Foreign Policy and War

Scholars of American history and politics today say that in the coming Century this country will no longer dominate the world as a superpower.[1] It will, however, have an important role to play with other great powers, for example, China and India as well as Russia. As the United States finds its place in the changing community of nations, five characteristics of its foreign policy can be seen in the choices it made in the Twentieth Century. They are: support for collective security, nuclear non-proliferation, trade agreements, economic and military aid to other nations in support of American objectives, and resolving hostilities in hot spots.

The past century has seen a vast extension and sophistication of American foreign policy as it learned to deal with the real world. Woodrow Wilson said to a friend on his Inauguration Day that he hoped his Presidency would not have to cope with foreign affairs because he was not at all prepared to lead the nation in that area. When the country needed a leader, though, he was ready. The isolationism of the '20s and '30s was dispelled with the Second World War when people realized that this country had to relate to other nations in a positive way. Retreat into purely national and local concerns would not secure peace.

During the First World War, Wilson himself saw the big picture: some kind of council of nations was necessary to work through the disputes that inevitably arise between nation-states. Moreover, certain values like the political right of self-determination of colonial peoples emerged in European social thought and political discourse. Wilson supported this principle. The colonial powers, Britain, France, the Netherlands, Germany, Spain and Portugal had reached the point where their colonies in Asia, Africa and South America had become a burden and some of them were clamoring for independent status. The United States was also a colonial power during Wilson's Administration; it acquired the Philippine Islands in the Spanish-American War of 1898. Puerto Rico and Cuba had been given their independence by Spain. The Hawaiian Islands, not colonies of Spain, were acquired as a Territory by the United States; they obtained Statehood in 1959. The Philippines, which had been a significant military resource for the United States in the Second World War, received its independence after the War. Puerto Rico, meanwhile, gradually became a commonwealth of the United States, with its own self-government. There continues to be talk of statehood for Puerto Rico.

Herbert Hoover was committed to the concept of the League of Nations, but was not President when the serious policy discussions were held at the end of the First World War, and when he came into office in 1929 he had to cope with the Great Depression. The American stock markets collapsed in October, seven months after he took the oath of office as President. A decade earlier, however, Hoover's reorganized Commerce Department had strengthened the commercial relations with other nations, promoted trade and dealt with tariff issues.

American foreign policy was led by Franklin Roosevelt in the '30s and early '40s, with the substantial help of Cordell Hull, who served as Secretary of State for eleven years. He helped the President work with such issues as the Neutrality Acts and later the Lend-Lease program of military hardware to Britain in exchange for the right of the United States to use certain of their bases. Hull is called the "Father of the United Nations," who drafted the concept of a United Nations organization which would have sufficient power and resources to be effective in keeping world peace. Ill health forced him to resign as Secretary of State, but he attended the San Francisco Conference as one of the American delegates. The Conference adopted a Charter of the UN. Cordell Hull received the Nobel Prize for Peace for his work to form the structure of the UN. By this time, the United States was committed to the concept of collective security as visualized by Woodrow Wilson in 1919 and has supported the United Nations ever since.

America was blessed with talented people in the mid-century when they were needed. General George Marshall was appointed Secretary of State by Harry Truman; he developed a financial assistance plan for post-war Europe which had been devastated by the Second World War. The Marshall Plan is credited with having been a major factor in the restoration of Europe. Truman himself was a substantial foreign policy leader for the Western powers in the post-war world when he used aid to Greece and Turkey as an arm to his foreign policy initiatives. This policy of giving aid to friendly countries to advance American interests as well as to help them became a fixture of the nation's foreign policy. The United States undertook alliances which involved some economic aid but largely military assistance in Southeast Asia, Africa, and the Pacific.

American policy regarding the possible proliferation of nuclear technology was developed during the Kennedy Administration when the President was able to sell the idea of a Limited Nuclear Test-Ban Treaty to the Soviet Union and other countries. The Senate ratified it in 1963. That treaty began a history of international efforts to deal with the possibility of irresponsible use of such weapons. After years of negotiations within the United Nations, this country agreed to a Comprehensive Nuclear Non-Proliferation Treaty in 1968. At the beginning of the Twenty-first Century, this subject is viewed by many in government as one of the most important issues the country faces in light of the terrorist movements around the world.

Other major contributors to America's position of dominance in the Western world during the Cold War were Henry Kissinger and President Nixon whom Kissinger served as both National Security Adviser and as Secretary of State. Nixon himself wanted to make his mark as a foreign policy President, and Kissinger helped him achieve that goal. Presidents Jimmy Carter, Ronald Reagan and George H.W. Bush each accomplished significant goals in international relations. Carter brought about a settlement between Israel and Egypt, Reagan carried out the final negotiations with the Soviet Union, and Bush, who served in a number of foreign policy capacities before he became President, had regular contact with the leaders of other nations during his Presidency. From those relationships he had no difficulty gaining the support of many governments when Saddam Hussein invaded Kuwait. Finally, he had personal contacts with King Fahd and other leaders of Saudi Arabia.

The United States under President Clinton's leadership helped resolve the sporadic but long-standing war of ethnic groups in the Balkans. He appointed former Senator George Mitchell to mediate the decades-long religious war in Northern Ireland which finally was resolved and is peaceful today. Clinton also tried to bring the Israelis and the Palestinians together to resolve the issues in their numerous disputes but could not bring about peace in the Middle East. Nor could George W. Bush. Clinton completed the NAFTA trade agreement sought by both Democratic and Republican Presidents for two decades before his Administration.

Overall, the Presidents of the Twentieth Century obtained and preserved a role for America as a world leader, and later as the sole Superpower. Because of this leadership, the world looked to the United States to promote peace and provide resources to the poor nations, to set a democratic model for other, especially emerging, nations to follow.

The American people want no war. Often, however, they could not avoid it, either because they were attacked in one form or another or the President in office found it necessary to defend the United States by preventing another nation from taking some action harmful to this country.

Persistent Social Stresses

Racism has been the elephant in the living room of American society for more than 200 years. People don't talk about it as a blight on the society, don't admit it to themselves or to others. Through much of the Twentieth Century, whites found it difficult to socialize with blacks because they saw a class line dividing them. From top to bottom, white racism dominated the culture. Presidents like Woodrow Wilson, a Southerner, and Dwight Eisenhower, a Kansan, were known to be racist and others may have harbored such attitudes but let inaction about race be their choice rather than taking an aggressive posture on this problem. Wilson segregated the federal government, removing blacks from federal employ when he was President. The government stayed racially segregated until Herbert Hoover became President. Hoover made a point of hiring blacks for government jobs. Harry Truman took an active role in promoting fairness not only by desegregating the military services but also by appointing a committee of African Americans to study and recommend action to him. When the committee reported back to him, he proceeded to put into effect what recommendations he could as President in the late 1940s, and for the rest he kept issues open until they could become part of civil rights legislation two decades later.

Eisenhower respected the law concerning school desegregation and sent a military force to secure the integration of the Central School in Little Rock, Arkansas. But Eisenhower may not have been able to muster within himself the positive attitude that would have been necessary to lead the American people to see the need for school integration. He acted in Little Rock to enforce the law proclaimed in *Brown vs Board of Education of Topeka.* The public has been slow to accept racial integration even after the Civil Rights Acts of the 1960s pointed to a new direction for American society.

However, through the Twentieth Century black leaders like Martin Luther King, Jr., Thurgood Marshall, Jesse Jackson, Andrew Young, and a growing number of black mayors in the nation's cities and among members of Congress have taught and led new generations of blacks to use the opportunities available to them, particularly in education. Educational institutions also have broadened their admission policies to be more inclusive as laws have required them to do. By 2008, an African-American candidate became the Democratic Party's nominee for President. His election as the 44th President of the United States was seen by many as vindication for the people who worked long and hard to bring about racial justice based on inter-racial respect.

The social stresses of racial difference sometimes have become compounded with the efforts of new immigrants, some in the country illegally, to settle in America's big cities. There is anger about the illegals based on the feeling that they have no right to be in the country. Moreover, they appear to be taking jobs away from

American citizens. In fact, many of the illegal immigrants get jobs Americans will not take, such as yard work, housecleaning and other menial jobs. A final complaint about these immigrants is that they cannot speak English, and don't seem to be learning it after they have been in the country for a while. In the absence of changes in the immigration law to provide an orderly process of earned citizenship, the government found itself in the position of having to enforce existing laws regarding deportation. Government agents undertook to raid manufacturing and other business firms, find and arrest illegal immigrants and deport them. This has caused much grief for families that are broken up; children who were born in the United States are legal citizens, but their parents are not. Separating the children from their parents is a major social abuse. At this writing, there is no solution planned for the distress current policies inflict on illegal immigrants. Instead, there is construction of a fence and barricade to keep the illegal immigrants from Mexico out.

In 2007, President Bush proposed to Congress a bill that would have eased the immigration problem by providing for earned citizenship, which included a requirement that the illegal immigrant pay a fine for having violated American law. An immigrant who did not want to stay in this country could become temporarily a guest worker, but would have to leave thereafter. In an anti-illegal furor, many Americans raged at Congress when it debated the bill; that body simply stopped consideration and the bill died.

Among some white people there is fear that people of color of all races will in time take away control of the nation from whites. This feeling has appeared at other times in the past, but gradually there is more acceptance of blacks and people of color in government and in many other areas of society. This is seen in the arts, literature, sports, and many social organizations. Especially, this has been seen in the year 2008 with the election of Barack Obama as President. It followed several years when significant black leaders were appointed to Cabinet posts or chief posts in the military services. Secretary of

State Colin Powell was followed in that office by Condoleeza Rice who had been serving as the President's National Security Advisor.

Through leadership, not only of the President but by leaders in a variety of organizations both political and social, this fear can be ameliorated. Americans, like people the world over, come to accept values that their leaders embrace.

POSTSCRIPT
December, 2008

By October, 2008, observers could see the denouement of government by the current conservative ideology. A major financial crisis struck not only in the United States but in financial systems around the world. Experts talked of a variety of causes: the proliferation of sub-prime mortgages in the United States by lenders who did not properly judge the borrowers as to their ability to pay on them, the loss of confidence in the investment banking sector which caused a number of them to go bankrupt or to be sold to other institutions. Some were bailed out by the United States government but this did little to give the average person confidence either in the markets or in the government. People feared that they would lose their savings in banks, and those who invested in 401(k) or other retirement accounts feared that the precipitous fall of the stock market threatened their life savings.

The roots of the crash and the recession that followed it were in false economic principles followed by some conservatives in and out of government since Ronald Reagan was President in the 1980s. They announced that "government is the problem," that taxes should be lowered, a policy of the Bush Administration in the face of the enormous costs that were being incurred by the two wars, one in Iraq and the other in Afghanistan. The lowering of taxes since 2001 only increased the government deficit, and thereby the already enormous national debt. Other myths actually believed by important government officials like the former chairman of the Federal Reserve Board of Governors of the Federal Reserve System, Alan Greenspan, contributed to the disaster. Three years retired from that post when the collapse occurred, Mr. Greenspan said that "he had put too much faith in the self-correcting power of free markets and had failed to anticipate the self-destructive power of wanton mortgage lending, leaving himself 'in a state of shocked disbelief.'"[1] The notion of the "invisible hand" that supposedly governed the market was an article of faith held by many people. But in fact, governments from Theodore Roosevelt through Woodrow Wilson and Franklin Roosevelt had instituted regulatory agencies and rules by which the "free market" should be governed. The conservatives interpreted the dictum of "government is the problem" to mean that many government regulations should be thrown out or at least drastically modified. Over time, the faith in deregulation became a mantra for the well-being of the country. So, such agencies as the Securities and Exchange Commission made some modification of its rules and became lax in its enforcement of the stock and bond markets.

In addition to the views expressed by conservatives, a statistical model called Value at Risk, or VaR, was developed in the 1990s and was used by J.P. Morgan. It was later shared with other financial institutions.[2] The model expresses the boundaries of risk in a portfolio as a single number after taking into account numerous variables including diversification, leverage and volatility. It has been popular among financial institutions because it proved to be true, reliable. It was used since the 1990s as an estimator of risk, but over the years it became misused. In the view of Joe Nocera, writing in an article about risk in the *New York Times*, "Maybe it would have helped if Wall Street hadn't turned VaR into something it was never meant to be."[3] Essentially, risk managers needed to look at the model as one of several measures one should use to understand a company's risk.

Nocera points out that there needs to be more transparency into evaluating risk. Without detailing here the aspects of this statistical measure, it is fair to say that its misuse had much to do with the bad estimates that financial leaders made in recent years and hence the important role it had in the financial meltdown.

As a balance for the conservatism in the '80s and '90s there did appear to be benefits for the average person in some of the deregulations. Airline fares came down with deregulation, the deregulation of the natural gas and electric power industries brought about more competition and lower costs to the customer. This balance could guide future Presidents if they are not confronted by disasters like war and economic recession. But even more important is that a President should not become convinced that some ideology about the economy works in all cases and will promote the well-being of the American people. The public, and especially businesses, must understand that a balanced economy requires a degree of regulation. There is greed and bad judgment lurking in the minds of many people and a civilized society requires personal restraint. Having more of everything is not what makes people happy. If it were, Americans would be the happiest people in the world. Instead the acquisitive society promotes ever more dissatisfaction and the behavior that goes with it.

Americans also should think about the kind of President the country needs to provide for the common defense and promote the general welfare. It's an old question, what makes a good President, what makes a good leader. In this country, with its diverse society and its many needs and wants, a President needs vigor and good health. He or she needs a good education, best realized when a person continues to learn for the rest of his or her life. Openness to experience, not the closure of the mind at some point in the maturing process, is vital. Openness to people around him and in the far reaches of the world is an important part of his education as well.

The President needs to be ready to act when a decision is necessary, and he needs to know when that point is reached in the political system in which he functions. He must respect our form of government, not always easy when a President must confront Congress and the vagaries of its wishes in the processing of legislation. On these measures, no President will be perfect, but some will stand the test of time and history will show that their service to the country promoted the well-being of its people. Much depends on the view of the Presidency of the man or woman who takes the oath of office on Inauguration Day.

BIBLIOGRAPHY

Ambrose, Stephen E. *Eisenhower: Soldier and President*. New York, Simon & Schuster, 1990.

Anderson, Judith Icke, *William Howard Taft An Intimate History*, New York, W.W. Norton & Co., 1981.

Beschloss, Michael, *The Conquerors: Roosevelt, Truman and the Destruction of Hitler's Germany, 1941-1945*, New York, Simon & Schuster, 2002.

Bourne, Peter G. *Jimmy Carter*, Scribner, A Lisa Drew Book, New York, 1997.

Brands, H.W. *Woodrow Wilson*, New York, Times Books, American Presidents Series, 2003.

Burner, David, *Herbert Hoover A Public Life,* New York, Alfred A. Knopf, 1979

Burns, James MacGregor, *Roosevelt: The Lion and the Fox*, New York, Harcourt, Brace & World, Inc., 1956.

Bush, George, *All The Best, My Life In Letters And Other Writings*, New York, Scribner, 1999.The letters of George H.W. Bush, the first President Bush.

Caro, Robert A. *The Years of Lyndon Johnson, Master of the Senate*, New York, Alfred A. Knopf, 2002.

_____*The Years of Lyndon Johnson, The Path to Power*, New York, Vintage Books, 1983.

Clinton, Bill, *My Life*, New York, Alfred A. Knopf, 2004.

Coll, Steve, *The Bin Ladens, An Arabian Family in the American Century*, New York, The Penguin Press, 2008.

Dolan, Chris J., Frendreis, John, and Tatalovich, Raymond, *The Presidency and Economic Policy*, Lanham, Md., Rowman & Littlefield Publishers, 2008.

Ferrell, Robert H. ed. *Harry S. Truman & The Bomb A Documentary History*, Worland Wyoming, High Plains Publishing Co. 1996.

Frank, Thomas, *The Wrecking Crew, How Conservatives Rule*, New York, Henry Holt & Co., 2008.

Friedman, Milton *Capitalism and Freedom*, Chicago, University of Chicago Press, 1962.

Friedman, Thomas, *The World is Flat, A Brief History of the Twenty-First Century*, New York, Farrar, Straus and Giroux, 2005.

Fromkin, David, *In the Time of the Americans, The Generation That Changed America's Role in the World*, New York, Alfred A. Knopf, 1995.

Gardner, Michael R. *Harry Truman and Civil Rights, Moral Courage and Political Risks*, Carbondale, Southern Illinois University Press, 2002.

Halberstam, David, *The Best and the Brightest*, New York, Random House, 1972.

Hamilton, Nigel, *Bill Clinton, Mastering the Presidency*, New York, Public Affairs, Perseus Books Group, 2007.

Harbaugh, William Henry, *The Life and Times of Theodore Roosevelt*, New York, Collier Books, 1963.

Heckscher, August, *Woodrow Wilson, A Biography*, New York, Charles Scribner's Sons, 1991.

Herring, George C. *From Colony to Superpower U.S. Foreign Relations Since 1776* Oxford, New York, Oxford University Press, Inc., 2008

Kissinger, Henry *White House Years*, Boston, Little Brown & Co., 1979.

Krugman, Paul, *The Conscience of a Liberal*, New York, W.W. Norton & Co., 2007.

Link, Arthur S. *Woodrow Wilson and the Progressive Era*, New York, Hasrper & Row, 1954.

Mulder, John M. *Woodrow Wilson The Years of Preparation*, Princeton, Princeton University Press, 1978.

Nixon, Richard M. *The Memoirs of Richard Nixon* New York, Grosset and Dunlap, 1978.

Nocera, Joe, "Risk Mismanagement," *New York Times Magazine*, January 4, 2009, p. 25 et seq.

Schlesinger, Arthur, M. Jr. *The Imperial Presidency*, Boston, Houghton Mifflin Co., 1973.

Smith, Richard Norton, *An Uncommon Man, The Triumph of Herbert Hoover*, New York, Simon and Schuster, 1984.

Smith, Adam, *An Inquiry Into the Nature and Causes of the Wealth of Nations*, 1776.

Strauss, Leo and Joseph Cropsey, *History of Political Philosophy*, Chicago, Rand McNally & Co., 1969.

Walker, Martin, *The President We Deserve, Bill Clinton: His Rise, Falls, and Comebacks*, New York, Crown Publishers, 1996.

Weisberg, Jacob, *The Bush Tragedy*, New York, Random House, 2008.

Wilson, Woodrow, *The New Freedom*, Project Gutenberg EBook of the New Freedom by Woodrow Wilson, www.gutenberg.net.

Woodward, Bob, *The War Within, A Secret White House History 2006-2008*, New York, Simon & Schuster, 2008.

Zakaria, Fareed *The Post-American World*, New York, W.W. Norton, 2008.

NOTES

The Economy in 1900

1 Smith, Adam, *An Inquiry Into The Nature And Causes Of The Wealth of Nations*, 1776.

2 Sumner, William Graham, *What Social Classes Owe to Each Other*, New York, Harper & Brothers, 1883.

3 *U.S. v United States Steel*, 251 US 417 (1920).

4 *U.S. v Aluminum Co. of America*, 148F2d 416; 148 F2d at 421 (1945).

Theodore Roosevelt

1 Harbaugh, William Henry, *The Life and Times of Theodore Roosevelt* New York, Collier Books, 1963, p. 16.

2 Ibid., p. 19

3 Ibid. pp. 54-55.

4 Ibid., p.85.

5 Ibid., p. 69.

6 Ibid., pp. 230-232.

7 Ibid., pp. 243-244.

8 Ibid., pp. 250-251

9 *Lochner v New York*, 198 U.S. 45 (1905).

10 *Muller v Oregon*, 208 U.S. 412 (1908).

11 Harbaugh Op.Cit., pp.194-195.

12 Ibid., pp. 212-213.

13 Ibid., p. 180.

William Howard Taft

1 Harbaugh, Op. Cit., p. 341.

2 Internet, Google, William Howard Taft Biography.

3 Internet, Google, William Howard Taft Biography.

4 Anderson, Judith Icke, *William Howard Taft An Intimate History*, New York, W.W. Norton & Co., 1981, p. 238.

Woodrow Wilson

1 Brands, H.W. *Woodrow Wilson*, New York, Times Books, American Presidents Series, 2003, p. 3.

2 Ibid., p. 10.

3 Mulder, John M. *Woodrow Wilson The Years of Preparation*, Princeton, Princeton University Press, 1978, p. 277.

4 Address to joint session of Congress April 8, 1913.

5 Wilson, Woodrow, *The New Freedom, A Call for the Emancipation of the Generous Energies of a People*, Project Gutenberg EBook of The New Freedom by Woodrow Wilson, www.gutenberg.net, pp.93-94.

6 Brands, Op. Cit. p. 59.

7 Ibid., p. 89.

8 Ibid., p. 98.

9 Ibid., pp. 115-116.

10 Ibid., pp. 119-120

11 Ibid., p.129.

The Progressives

1 Link, Arthur S. *Woodrow Wilson and the Progressive Era*, New York, Harper & Row, 1954, p.16.

2 Roosevelt, Theodore, "A Confession of Faith," speech to Bull Moose Party Convention, upon his nomination for the Presidency, 1912.

3 Strauss, Leo and Joseph Cropsey, eds., *History of Political Philosophy*, Chicago, Rand McNally & Co., 1969, pp. 697-722.

Warren G. Harding

1 www.whitehouse.gov/history/presidents/wh

2 Herring, George C. *From Colony to Superpower: U.S. Foreign Relations Since 1776*, Oxford, New York, Oxford University Press, Inc. 2008, p.436.

3 Ibid., p. 439.

4 Ibid., p. 442.

5 Ibid., p. 443

6 Ibid., p. 443

John Calvin Coolidge

1 www.whitehouse.gov/history/presidents/cc 30.html – 17k

2 Internet, whitehouse.gov/history/presidents

3 Idem..

Herbert Clark Hoover

1 Burner, David, *Herbert Hoover: A Public Life*, New York, Alfred A. Knopf, 1979, p. 289.

2 Smith, Richard Norton, *An Uncommon Man, The Triumph of Herbert Hoover*, Mew York, Simon and Schuster, 1984, pp.73-76.

3 Ibid., p.79.

4 Ibid., p. 93

5 Ibid., p. 116.

6 Ibid. p. 110.

7 Ibid., p. 119.

8 Ibid., p. 118.

9 Ibid., p. 119.

10 Ibid., p. 118.

11 Ibid., p. 119.

12 Burner, Op. Cit. p. 245.

13 Ibid., p. 247.

14 Smith, Op. Cit, p. 109.

15 Ibid.,, p. 108.

16 Burner, Op Cit, p. 253.

17 Smith, Op Cit, p. 128.

18 Ibid., p. 108.

19 Ibid., p. 114

20 Ibid, p. 108.

21 Ibid., p. 133.

22 Ibid., p. 108.

23 Burner, Op Cit, p. 216.

Franklin Delano Roosevelt

1 Burns, James MacGregor, *Roosevelt: The Lion and the Fox*, New York, Harcourt, Brace & World, Inc., 1956, p. 194.

2 Ibid., p. 169.

3 Ibid., p. 181.

4 Ibid., pp. 217-219.

5 Ibid., p. 233.

6 Ibid., p. 311.

7 Ibid., pp. 303-314.

8. Ibid., pp. 330-334.

9 Ibid., p. 335.

10 Fromkin, David, *In the Time of the Americans*, New York, Alfred a. Knopf, 1995, p.461.

11 Ibid., pp. 481; Burns, Op Cit, pp.469-470.

12 Internet, Cordell Hull Biography, Nobel Peace Prize, 1945.

Harry S. Truman

1 Fromkin, Op Cit, p. 488.

2 Ferrell, Robert H. ed. *Harry S. Truman and the Bomb, A Documentary History*, Worland Wyoming, High Plains Publishing Co., 1996, p. 102.

3 Ibid., p. 32.

4 Ibid., p. 2.

5 Ibid., p. 37.

6 Fromkin, Op. Cit. p. 480.

7 Ibid., p.505.

8 Ibid., p. 504.

9 Kissinger, *White House Years*, Boston, Little, Brown & Co., 1979, p. 62.

10 Gardner, Michael R. *Harry Truman and Civil Rights, Moral Courage and Political Risks,* Carbondale, Southern Illinois University Press, 2002, p. 51.

11. *Youngstown Sheet and Tube Co. v Sawyer,* 343 U.S. 579 (1952).

Fear of Communism

1 Fromkin, Op. Cit. p. 493.

2 *Dennis v United States* 341 U.S. 494 (1951).

3 *Yates v United States* 354 U.S. 298 (1957)

Dwight D. Eisenhower

1 Fromkin, Op Cit p. 43

2 Ibid., p. 283.

3 Herring, Op Cit, p. 656.

4 Idem

5 Ibid., p. 657

6 Ibid., p. 659.

7 Ibid., p. 663.

8 Ibid., p. 669.

9 Ibid, p. 676.

10 Dolan, Chris J., John Frendreis and Raymond Tatalovich, *The Presidency and Economic Policy,* Lanham, Rowman & Littlefield Publishers, Inc., 2008, p.170.

The Economy in Mid-Century

1 Krugman, Paul, *The Conscience of a Liberal,* New York, W.W. Norton & Co., 2007, p. 70.

2 Ibid., p. 58.

3 Burns, Op Cit, p. 143, 246.

4 Friedman, Milton, *Capitalism and Freedom*, Chicago, University of Chicago Press. 1962. Chapter 1, "The Relation Between Economic Freedom and Political Freedom," pp. 7-17.

John Fitzgerald Kennedy

1 Ambrose, Stephen E. *Eisenhower, Soldier and President*, New York, Simon & Schuster, 1990, p. 553.

2 Schlesinger, Arthur M., J. *The Imperial Presidency*, Boston, Houghton Mifflin Co., 1973, pp.173-176.

3 Internet, Wikipedia, "Cuban Missile Crisis."

4 Halberstam, Op Cit, pp. 243-245.

Lyndon Baines Johnson

1 Caro, Robert A., *The Years of Lyndon Johnson Master of the Senate*, New York, Alfred A. Knopf, 2002, p. 725.

2 Ibid., p. 760.

3 *Civil Rights Cases*109 U.S. 3 (1883), et cetera; final paragraph: "The 1964 act's public accommodations provision was based on the Commerce Clause" because there had been doubt whether Congress could legislate in the area of civil rights.

4 Civil Rights Act 1964, Pub. Law 88-352 78 Stat.241, July 2, 1964.

5 Dirksen role: Civil Rights Act 1964 Wikipedia.

6 www.whitehouse.gov/history/presidents/lj 36.html – 18k.

7 www.guardian.co.uk/world/2002/May 19/the observer - 83k

8 Halberstam, Op Cit, p. 592

9 Ibid., p. 596

10 Ibid., p. 595

11 Ibid., p. 596.

12 Ibid., p. 597.

13 Ibid, p. 599.

14 Dolan, Op. Cit., pp. 258-260.

Richard M. Nixon

1 Schlesinger, Arthur M., Jr. *The Imperial Presidency*, Boston, Houghton Mifflin Co., 1973, p. 193.

2 Chambers, Whittaker *Witness*, New York, Random House, 1952.

3 Kissinger, Op Cit, p.78.

4 Ibid., pp. 11-12.

5 Ibid., pp.26-28.

6 Nixon, Richard, New York, *The Memoirs of Richard Nixon*, Grosset & Dunlap, 1978, pp 492-493.

7 Ibid., pp. 518-520.

8 Ibid., p. 521.

9 Ibid., p. 521

10 Kissinger, Op Cit, p. 164.

11 Idem.

12 Ibid., p. 165.

13 Nixon, Op Cit, p. 346.

14 Ibid., p. 242.

15 Ibid., p 677, pp. 680-681.

16 Ibid., p. 696.

17 Ibid., p. 692

18 Kissinger, Op Cit, pp. 986n, 1255.

19 Nixon, Op Cit, pp 515-521.

20 Ibid., pp 485-489.

21 Ibid., 487-489

22 Ibid., p. 487.

23 Ibid., pp. 489-490.

24 Nixon, Op Cit, p. 620.

25 Ibid., p. 876

26 Ibid., p. 880.

27 Ibid., pp 888-889

28 Ibid., p. 880

29 Kissinger, Op Cit, p. 66.

30 Ibid., pp. 1475-1476.

James Earl Carter

1 Bourne, Peter G. *Jimmy Carter*, New York, Scribner, 1997, pp. 374-375.

2 Ibid., p. 375.

3 Ibid., pp. 375-377.

4 Ibid., p. 445.

5 Ibid., pp. 440, 449, 381-382.

6 Ibid., pp.401-411.

Ronald Reagan

1 Reeves, Richard, *President Reagan, The Triumph of Imagination*, p. xvii.

2 Walker, Martin, *The President We Deserve, Bill Clinton: His Rise, Falls, and Comebacks*, New York, Crown Publishers, 1996, p. 23.

3 Herring, Op Cit p. 873

4 Ibid., p. 897

5 Reeves, Op Cit p. 482.

6 Herring, Op Cit, pp. 898-899.

7 Reeves, Op Cit pp. 276-277.

8 Ibid., pp. 221-222.

9 Reeves, Op Cit, p.376.

10 Ibid., p. 377.

11 Ibid. p. 374.

12 Reeves, Op Cit p. 399.

13 Ibid., p. 400.

George H.W. Bush

1 Weisberg, Jacob, *The Bush Tragedy*, New York, Random House, 2008, pp. 31-32.

2 Ibid., p. 33.

3 Ibid., p. 48.

4 Bush, George, *All the Best, My Life in Letters and Other Writings*, New York, Scribner, 1999, p. 179.

5 Weisberg, Op Cit, p. 58.

6 Coll, Steve, *The Bin Ladens, An Arabian Family in the American Century*, New York, Penguin Press, 2008, p. 9.

7 Ibid., pp. 14-15.

8 This important statement is from author's memory.

9 Bush, Op Cit, pp. 505-506

10 Ibid., p. 483

11 Beschloss, Michael, American Presidents Series, Internet Biographies George Bush, "Character Above All", p. 6.

William Clinton

1 Clinton, Bill, *My Life*, New York, Alfred A. Knopf, 2004, p. 114.

2 Ibid., p. 444.

3 Ibid., p. 721

4 Ibid., 546.

5 Ibid., p. 540.

6 Ibid. p. 546.

7 Herring, Op.Cit. pp. 924, 925-31.

8 Friedman, Thomas L. *The World is Flat A Brief History of the Twenty-First Century*, New York, Farrar, Straus and Giroux, 2005.

9 Herring, Op. Cit., p. 875.

10 Ibid., p. 924.

11 Ibid., p. 930.

12 Clinton, Op. Cit. pp. 784-785.

13 Ibid., pp. 911-916.

14 Ibid. pp. 610-611.

George Walker Bush

1 Weisberg, Jacob, *The Bush Tragedy*, New York, Random House, 2008.

2 Ibid., p. xxvi.

3 Ibid., p. xxvii

4 Woodward, Bob *The War Within, A Secret White House History 2006-2008*, New York, Simon & Schuster, 2008, p. 136.

5 Ibid., p. 134.

Conclusion

1 Zakaria, Fareed, *The Post-American World*, New York, W.W. Norton & Co., 2008.

Postscript

1 *New York Times*, Oct. 24, 2008; Greenspan, p. 1.

2 Nocera, Joe, "Risk Mismanagement," *New York Times Magazine*, January 4, 2009, p. 25.

3 Ibid., p. 50.

About the Author

Elizabeth Warren is a retired college professor of Political Science who continues to find the study of government exciting. Of particular interest today are the changes that are occurring in American society and their impact on our government's policies.

Warren took her graduate work fifteen years after receiving her B.A. degree in History from Bryn Mawr College. She received her Master's degree from the University of Kansas and concluded her work for the doctorate in Political Science at the University of Nebraska. She also went into active politics in local government, serving as a Trustee and then Mayor of the Village of Glencoe, Illinois, a suburb of Chicago.

She has published books on subjects as disparate as the impact of the Gautreaux v Chicago Housing Authority court decision and the relationships between religion and politics. She also wrote a biography of a 19th Century Quaker who was a leader in the development of the Society of Friends in the Midwest.

Warren's husband was a Sears executive, and she has four grown daughters.

6825235R0

Made in the USA
Lexington, KY
23 September 2010